Malta's Mediterranean Cuisine

By Rainer Mitze

Malta's Mediterranean Cuisine

UMSCHAU :

Design and Typeset by
juhu media, Susanne Dölz, Bad Vilbel

Manufactured by
Lithotronic media Gmbh, Frankfurt/Main

Food photography by
Foodfoto Holz, Cologne

We would like to thank Ms Swantje Klotz from the Malta Tourism Authority in Frankfurt for her friendly assistance in the composition of the introduction to Malta's Mediterranean Cuisine as well as for the rich choice of photo material supplied by the MTA.

Printed in Italy by
LEGO, Vicenza

ISBN 3-86528-214-8

Visit us in the internet under:
www.umschau-buchverlag.de

Content

Typical Maltese cooking – a potpourri of cultures

Mhux bogħod mid-dar jekk mhux bogħod mill-kcina

»If you're not far from the kitchen, then you're not far from home«

The Islands of Malta and Gozo have been exposed to different rulers who reigned over the islands, each leaving their distinctive mark over the centuries. This fusion of customs became the fundamental element to strongly influence the customs and traditions that developed; a unique element that can be felt also architecturally and linguistically.
This tiny archipelago encountered and adopted the cooking customs of the Arabs, North Africans, Sicilians, the British and those of the Knights of the Cross, thus dishes range from Turkish honey to British pies and pastries. The Italian and North African influences are probably the most significant. The Maltese tend to cook and eat at home with their families. Recipes are treasured within the family, handed down from generation to generation; it follows that Maltese cuisine still represents centuries of Mediterranean farmhouse cooking that has retained its unique character.
Rural cooking is deeply rooted and has changed very little over the years. Typical dishes, just to name a few, are vegetable soups such as the »widow's soup« (soppa ta'l-armla) and stews, unleavened bread baked in a brick oven, goat's cheese and potatoes. Middle-class cooking has been predominantly influenced by the Mediterranean milieu. »Timpana« (a baked pasta dish with a flaky pastry top) is similar to a Sicilian »timballo«, stuffed paprikas and aubergines stem from the coast of Asia Minor (modern Turkey). The two most popular desserts »ħelva« and »imqaret«, originate from the Ottoman empire and Tunisia, most probably these were introduced into Maltese cooking by seamen, Muslim prisoners or wandering Jews.
Maltese cooking has always featured olives, capers, garlic, herbs together with a rich array of seasonal fruit and vegetables.

Msida harbour

The first inhabitants of Malta came from Sicily and southern Italy over 6000 years ago. They built around 40 of the famous Megalithic temples which are spread over the island, today these are the oldest freestanding, manmade buildings.

Typical local produce

Delicious fruit

The Maltese islands offer a large variety of exquisite fresh fruit such as watermelons, cherries, plums, pears, peaches and nectarines.

Maltese oranges are quite particular and deserve to be mentioned. They are sweet, small, and very juicy with a thin peel. There are many types of oranges however blood oranges are probably the most delicious. Since bitter oranges are more robust these are grown alongside the sweeter oranges to help support their growth. The Maltese use these bitter oranges to make marmalade a well as »Ilma Żahar«, an aromatic orange-blossom distillate used to flavour almonds and other sweets. It is also served with coffee to aid digestion. »Ilma Żahar« is also regarded as a traditional household medicine against stomach problems when added to black tea or camomile tea. Orange-peel extracts along with several herbs are part of the secret formula for the bittersweet Maltese fizzy drink called »Kinnie«, a tasty and refreshing drink without any added preservatives sought by adults and children alike.

Another item not to be missed is local figs. The most popular are »bajtar ta' San Gwann« (St. John's fig), that ripens at the end of June, the small green »farkizzan« harvested in July as well as the »parsott« that can be eaten until the end of September.

Honey

Locally produced honey known as »għasel« in Maltese is a speciality not to be missed. We recommend every island visitor to at least try some of this pure nectar. The Maltese make two sorts of honey: either by bees that feed on »Silla«

From 870 until 1070, Malta, Gozo and Comino were under Arabian rule. The Arabians not only created a functioning administration, but also a productive agricultural system, which was operated with the help of irrigation systems and terraced fields.

From 700 BC Malta was influenced by the Phoenicians, who used Malta as a base on their long trading trips. Relics of this time, such as the shape of the Maltese »dgħajsa« or fishing boats, with their typical Phoenician eye on the bow, can still be found in Maltese culture today. The Maltese are very superstitious and as the eye on the fishing boat is believed to protect the fishermen from disasters such as distress at sea. Hardly a fisherman sets out to sea in a boat without the eye painted on the bow.

(clover) or by bees that feed on »saghtar« (wild thyme). The latter has an extremely spicy taste.

Vegetables

Vegetables compliment each dish, adding that special touch; from courgettes (zucchini) and artichokes, cabbage and cauliflower, to sun-ripened tomatoes and potatoes each having a strong, distinctive taste. The Maltese islands possess very little rural land but every bit of fertile earth is put to use! The landscape is speckled with rubble walls built by local peasants to protect their fields and to prevent soil erosion.

Meat dishes

As there is no pastureland on the Maltese islands livestock is rare. Pigs, cattle, sheep and goats are kept in barns. Wild rabbits are also rare nowadays, so most of the rabbits – averaging around two million a year – are bred and farmed within households. The Maltese love their »fenek« (rabbit) and »fenkata« is regarded as the Maltese national dish. The traditional appetizer for this dish is spaghetti with a sauce made from pieces of the rabbit not used for the »fenkata«.
The Maltese also love »bragjoli«, a beef roll stuffed with bacon, garlic and parsley, as well as »pulpettun« (meat loaf) and »majjal filforn« (roast pork often roasted in the oven together with potatoes, onions and fennel seeds).

Fish

Fish plays by far a major role on the menu of this Mediterranean island. Fish is sold on Sunday mornings in the picturesque harbour of Marsaxlokk or at the daily fish market in Valletta. Any fish connoisseur would be elated by the large variety available. Depending on the time of year, one may find »spnotta« (bass), »dott« (stonebass), »ċerna« (grouper), »dentiċi« (dentex), »sargu« (white bream) as well as »trill« (trill) and sea urchins. Later in the year »pixxispad« (swordfish) and tuna are also caught.

In late summer »lampuka« (dorado – a type of gilthead) is abundantly in season. This tasty white fish is used to prepare a variety of dishes amongst which to bake pies called »torta tal-lampuki« – a scrumptious dish held to be the island's second national dish.

Sweet dishes

Most of the sweet dishes are of Sicilian origin and are usually eaten particularly on religious feast days. »Prinjulata«, a kind of butter-cream tart made of a sponge-biscuit base, pine-nuts, glacé cherries and chocolate is only available during carnival (a time of indulgence before Lent) whilst »kwarezimal« (Lent pastries) are only available during the fasting period between Ash Wednesday and Good Friday, primarily because they are baked without fat, eggs, and milk in adherence to the Roman Catholic Church regulations. »Zeppoli ta' San Guzepp«, are small doughnuts filled with ricotta, chocolate, glacé cherries and nuts. These are available on St. Joseph's Day, 19th March, one of Malta's national holidays. Easter is the time for »Figolli«, pastry filled with marzipan decorated with colourful icing and a chocolate egg. The pastry is cut into different shapes such as that of a fish or a lamb and according to mythology is offered to the Goddess of Fertility.

Maltese bread

The Maltese are especially proud of their delicious bread, which is traditionally baked in brick ovens. Typical Maltese farmer's bread »ħobża« is crisp on the outside and wonderfully light and airy on the inside. This »sour-dough« bread is made with leavened yeast left over from the previous day's baking.

Another favourite with the Maltese, following the »ħobża« is »ftira«, a flat, round loaf with a hole in the middle. It resembles the unleavened bread of the Eastern Mediterranean region. A tendency has developed during the last few years to bake »ftira« as flat as a pizza and then cover it with eggs, tomatoes, anchovies and capers.
Maltese hors d'oeuvres (starters) always include »galletti«, a wheat-flour bread baked into small, round, hard crackers. »galletti« is used as an accompaniment to the olive oil and enjoyed with »bigilla«, a paste consisting of thick beans and garlic.
Pastizzi (small, crisp pastries) are common everyday snacks. Two varieties are pastries filled with the soft, cream cheese we know as ricotta (»pastizzi talirkotta «) or filled with peas (»tal-Pizelli"). Since most bakeries or village

SEA-SALT PRODUCTION

Of course salt used in Maltese cooking is also produced locally. Salt pans can be found in Malta as well as in Gozo. In Gozo these are located in the picturesque landscape of the north down a beautiful scenic path along the pans by the coast. There you can see how seawater runs into the pans carved out from the typical chalk-sandstone. Salt gradually crystallizes as the water evaporates in the sun. The dried salt is dug out of the pans in late summer, usually around September, before the first rains.

bars make the pastizzi according to their own recipe, there are many variations. Pastizzi are great for taking along as a snack or on a picnic. The Maltese often enjoy two or three pastizzi as a second breakfast during their coffee break.

Capers and olives

Caper bushes drape over many old town walls, abundantly covered in buds that are later marinated to flavour various local dishes. During weekends Maltese families enjoy going out to pick capers, which they then pickle at home in a salt solution or in red vinegar. These pickled capers are later used in a large variety of dishes such as sauces and salads.

Olives thrive in Malta and Gozo. The harvest is made up by quality rather than quantity; the picked olives are then pickled or preserved in oil.

Olive oil is synonymous with the Mediterranean diet; this definitely applies to Maltese food. The olive oil industry flourished under the aegis of the Roman Empire, which is reflected in the names of places for example Żebbug (olive village) or Żejtun (oil village). In the early Middle Ages the olive oil industry decreased and eventually disappeared, so that this precious commodity had to be imported along with grain and other important merchandise.

In the year 2000 Mr. Sam Cremona bought an olive press and thus revived the lost art of pressing olives for their oil. For the first time in a thousand years, Maltese olive oil was produced.

Maltese extra virgin olive oil is genuine first cold press oil of the finest quality, low in acidity and rich with the flavour of green, peppery olives. This can be attributed to the excellent alkaline soil and long hours of sunshine, as well as to the fact that the olives are hand picked and pressed within a few hours of harvesting. The oil is stored in stainless steel vats before being filled into glass bottles and packed into cardboard boxes to prevent damage caused by exposure to light and air. The olive crop increases annually, thus the production of olive oil is becoming more and more significant. Cremora is in the process of acquiring the EU certification of organic production for the extra virgin olive oil.

Olive oil is also an important ingredient in preparing »Ħobz biż-żejt« (bread with oil) which is one of the most popular starters in Malta; it could even be considered a national dish. This starter consists of juicy, red tomatoes rubbed onto a thick slice of crispy Maltese bread and topped with mint, onions, sheep's cheese and anchovies – with delicious green olive oil added.

Dried tomatoes also have a strong placing in Maltese cooking. Traditionally sea-salt is scattered over fresh, ripe tomatoes which are then sun-dried. The dried tomatoes are preserved in local olive oil.

Viticulture in Malta

No Mediterranean meal is really complete without a glass of wine to complement it, and the wine produced on these islands is perfectly suited to the Maltese specialities.

Malta has a long wine-growing tradition, dating back to the Phoenician era.

Further development of wine cultivation depended on which occupying power reigned in Malta. After the Phoenicians came the Romans (A.D. 239). When the Roman Empire ceased to exert its influence, winegrowing declined during the time of the Arabian occupation, as alcohol was banned by the Islamic faith.

When the Maltese islands were transferred to the Order of the Knights of St. John of Jerusalem by King Charles V of Spain in 1530, they found the remaining vines in a pitiful condition. The knights, who came from the wine-producing countries of Europe,

»St. Paul's Estate« supplies the grapes for the very popular and excellent »Cheval Franc«.

immediately set about planting new vines and found that the mild Mediterranean climate offered ideal conditions for wine growing. Today there are four well-known and several small wineries. Farmers also make their own »house wines«, which can be purchased at the side of the road together with vegetables and honey, most without a label, or in rustic pubs and restaurants.

Since ancient times the islands have had three typical grape varieties: Ghirgentina and Gennuarua grapes are harvested to produce white wines and the Gellewza grape is grown for the red wine.

Nowadays Malta's leading wine producer is Marsovin, a brand name that stands for high-quality wines. This vintner's foundation

»Antonin Noir«, »Marnisi Red« and »Marnisi Rosé« are produced from grapes grown on the largest contiguous winegrowing area of »Marnisi« (en route to the fishing harbour of Marsaxlokk). Here the Cabernet Sauvignon, Cabernet Franc, Petit Verdot and Merlot grapes are grown.

The »Wardija Estate« grows the grapes for Malta's first sparkling wine, the »Cassar de Malte«. This wine is made using the »méthode traditionnelle«, the typical method used in France to produce champagne.

Chardonnay grapes used to make »Antonin Blanc« are harvested on the »Ramla l-Hamra Valley Estate« in Gozo.

stone was laid 1919 when Chev. Anthony Cassar founded the firm as A. & G. Cassar, a name that was changed to Marsovin in 1956. From the beginning, this family business has strongly influenced the development of wine production in Malta.

Malta's best wine is probably the »Grand Maître«, an outstanding red wine, which is pressed from the grapes of the small »Ghain Rihana Estate« which has a mere 1.1 ha. Each vintage is dedicated to one of the grand masters of the Order of the Knights of St. John. The first harvest was gathered in 1998 and high prices are already paid by connoisseurs.

Marsovin cellars

Marsovin was the first Maltese wine cellar to introduce the Cabernet Sauvignon grapes to the island. When the vintner planted them on their vineyards near Wardija, it was a historic step since this was the beginning of Malta´s superior vintage wines. The success of this wine demonstrated Malta´s potential for producing extraordinarily good wines. Encouraged by this success, more and more vines were planted which has considerably changed the landscape over the past decades. Many previously dry and infertile areas have now become thriving vineyards.

Partially, Malta's wines are grown on very small fields which are enclosed by stone-walls. These little vineyards can be found on the plains as well as on the mountain side terraces of Malta and Gozo, where they are sheltered from the wind by stone-walls.

Marsovin not only possesses its own vineyards, but also purchases grapes from over 400 wine-growers. The company produces both general wines and a selection of »Single Estate Wines«, these are wines made exclusively from the grapes harvested in a particular vineyard. Substantial investments were made in order to produce outstanding wines. Thus, over the past few years, Malta's winegrowing has shown extraordinary growth. With the support of the Maltese government more and more land is being cultivated. An example of this government assistance are the subsidiaries given to encourage the planting of grapes on land currently lying idle or being used to grow other crops.

The demand for these premium quality wines is growing steadily. Marsovin has responded by making their wines available to the Maltese, the Germans and the rest of Europe.

Liqueurs

You shouldn't leave the Islands without tasting Maltese liqueurs. Madalien Ltd, a local company dedicated to the production of high quality liqueurs offers a wide choice of liqueurs amongst which the Zeppi's range: A choice of traditional Maltese liqueurs made from old recipes dating back to the knights of Malta.

The original prickly pear liqueur »Bajtra liqueur« is one of the delicacies made from the opuntia ficus-indica commonly known as the prickly pear that was introduced towards the end of the 15th century to the Mediterranean region from the Americas.

Eventually it found its way to Malta and Gozo, where it has flourished and become part of the local landscape of the rubble-walled country side.

First used by the knights for its skin and its moisturizing property, the prickly pear, or Bajtra in Maltese, has lent its enticing fragrance and unique flavour to various local delicacies, not least Zeppi's Bajtra liqueur – to be enjoyed chilled or on ice, neat or as a long drink.

In days of old, honey was believed to be the cure to most maladies, and was added to grain spirits for medicinal purposes. This produced such a heart-warming liqueur that it became a Maltese tradition passed on and savoured from one generation to another.

Madalien Ltd, have borrowed and enhanced this tradition to produce a honey liqueur which their forefathers would have been proud of. Whether sipped on its own, ice cold, or with a dash of lemon, Zeppi's honey liqueur brings you years of tradition and bounty.

Anise, one of the oldest cultivated spices was already enjoyed by the early Egyptians, Greeks and Romans. Anisette liqueur has always been considered a rare delicacy served at wedding receptions and on special occasions. Made from a recipe that has been handed down through generations, this traditional Maltese liqueur boasts a concentration of aniseeds blended with local aromatic herbs. It can be enjoyed neat or as a refreshing long drink with water, lemonade, cola or tonic. This liqueur also blends beautifully with orange, pineapple or blackcurrant juices. A dash of Zeppi's Anisette liqueur added to black coffee is a unique reflection of Maltese Tradition.

›Il-Fatra‹ Foundation for Maltese Culinary Culture

The richness of a nation's culinary heritage is identified by its roots together with the influences of trade and economic growth throughout the passage of time.
›Il-Fatra‹ Foundation aims at promoting the uniqueness of Maltese Culinary Culture in that it is a marriage of Semitic roots and European influences, reaching a zenith in the 18th century, a culmination that arguably is yet to be surpassed. Promotion is to be achieved by developing teaching activities on sensory education and food culture through active participation. Other initiatives involve Taste Workshops, Conferences on culinary Heritage, and fun education through different mediums available.
Home to the foundation is ›1743 Ir-Razzett L-Antik Culinary and Conference Centre‹, a 400 year old milling farmhouse which has been restored, and today caters in 18th century slow food farmhouse cooking. It is located in the rural village of Qormi, reknown for its traditional bread making and rightfully identified as the bakers' village for more than 500 years.

The Venue ›1743‹ Ir-Razzett L-Antik

Situated in the medieval village of Qormi lies a 400-year-old farmhouse originally built to grind wheat into flour used to make Maltese bread by the village bakers. Today this farmhouse has been restored and transformed into the unique *›1743 Ir-Razzett l-Antik Culinary and Conference Centre‹*.

The ››Il-Fatra‹‹ foundation is located in a 400-year old mill-house

Combining together some of Malta's finest and oldest traditions and 600 years of culinary heritage, *›1743 Ir-Razzett l-Antik Culinary and Conference Centre‹* caters for the MICE business (Management, Incentive, Conference and Events) as well as diners who wish to be entertained in the venue's distinctive rustic ambiance.
With a dining capacity of 250 people, the venue offers a taste of Maltese traditions and farmhouse cooking, using old recipes handed down from the times of the Order of St John with all their glory, exotic spices and fabulous ingredients. With this in mind the kitchen fuses old and new methods of cooking, incorporating the art of marinating, slow food cooking and modern methods of preser-

vation to provide our guests with a unique taste of days of old and traditional farmhouse cooking.
The Culinary Centre features an underground cellar housing a wide selection of Maltese wines from different local producers and accessible by lift, a multi media exhibition showing the fortifications of the island and a conference room equipped with a PA System seating 150 persons theatre style.

This historic building with its fantastic rooms houses Rainer Mitze's new cookery school. Throughout cookery courses, the participants take an active part in the cooking and tasting, thus the star chef presents *his* Maltese cuisine. On the one hand he retains the traditional Maltese cuisine in all the facets we have described, but on the other hand he also gives this very original cuisine which has been handed down for generations a modern yet very individual touch by combining it with other culinary styles and by using products from other regions. Local Maltese ingredients naturally form the basis: lots of fresh fruit and vegetables are indispensable – Maltese figs and tomatoes are used in a number of recipes. Fish and rabbit are also included. The different cultures which have left their mark on Maltese cuisine can also be felt in the recipes of the chef, who has become wellknown through the German version of the TV programme »Ready, Steady, Cook«. His pasta recipes, for example, reflect the Italian influence, whereas the cakes, pastries and many desserts can be traced back to the Arab heritage.

Above all, the positive elements, landmarks of Mediterranean cuisine, such as the use of olive oil (best Maltese of course ...), gentle cooking, etc. are clearly recognizable. The special aspect of Rainer

In the family-style ambience of the »Ir-Razzett L'Antik«, waiters wear the traditional national costume and carry the dishes out to the wooden tables in wicker baskets.

Mitze's new Maltese cuisine is that he integrates other culinary styles and uses the traditional ingredients in an original way. A good example is his perfect combination of Maltese artichokes with truffles from Var in Southern France, another example is the refreshing gazpacho made with a crunchy ruccola or the preparation of Malta's most popular fish as Lampuki Tartar to be served with risotto.

The cookery courses are open and readily available to all holidaymakers who have become fans of Maltese cuisine during their stay on the archipelago, as well as for people with a passion for cooking who are interested in new culinary styles. The courses can be organised as an event for business people. After Rainer Mitze's »cooking students« have been launched into the secrets of modern Mediterranean cuisine, the results are enjoyed together with local drinks to compliment the meal, with Madalien liqueurs as an aperitif or digestif, Marsovin wines to round up the meal and the refreshing beers and Kinnie produced by Farsons.

Anyone wanting to try out their newly acquired cooking skills at home can buy all the necessary ingredients and drinks from the cookery school's gourmet shop – and of course support and suggestions are available in the recipes on the following pages. We hope all those who have

stayed at home enjoy trying them out too – and maybe they'll whet your appetite to get to know the new Maltese Mediterranean cuisine of Rainer Mitze!

◄ Rainer Mitze's new cookery college is located in the historic ambience of the »Ir-Razzette L'Antik«.

RECIPES

unless otherwise mentioned, all of the recipies are calculated 4 people (i.e. 4 servings)

STARTERS

Soups Salads Appetizers

Lampuki soup

For the fish stock

500 g fish bones
1 twig celery leaves
1 bay leaf
1/2 tsp dried thyme
1/2 tsp dried oregano
500 g lampuki pieces, skinned and boned
2 T black peppercorns

For the soup

200 g white bread, cut into cubes
1 large onion
3 large, ripe tomatoes
2 garlic cloves
6 T olive oil, cold pressed
10 peeled almonds
1 pinch saffron
salt
black pepper, freshly ground
1 pinch cinnamon

Place the fish bones, celery leaves, spices and 200g of the lampuki pieces into a saucepan. Crush the peppercorns and include them. Boil up the above ingredients in 1 l of water, close the lid and continue to boil for 15 minutes. Cover half of the white bread into cubes, put them in a cup and pour some of the stock over them.

Peel and chop the onion. Scald the tomatoes with boiling water to skin them and cut out the stalk-ends, halve the tomatoes and cut into cubes. Peel the garlic. Heat 2 tablespoons of olive oil and fry the onion, pressed garlic clove and the tomato pieces at medium heat for apx. 10 minutes.

Stir-fry the almonds in a pan (without fat) at medium heat until the roasted almonds give of a pleasant aroma. Remove the almonds from the pan and crush them with a pestle and mortar.

Cut the remaining garlic clove into small pieces and together with the saffron, add it to the almonds. Pound into a fine paste.
Strain the fish stock through a fine sieve and throw out the bones. Stir in 1 - 2 tablespoons of the fish stock into the paste.

Puree the fish (lampuki) and the soaked bread in the mixer, add a little fish stock if necessary. Boil up the mixture with the rest of the strained stock, add the almond mixture and boil everything for about 10 minutes.
Cut the remaining lampuki into little cubes and marinate in a tablespoon of olive oil for apx. 5 minutes. Meanwhile fry the rest of the bread in olive oil at a medium setting until they are golden-brown. Flavour the soup with salt, pepper and cinnamon.

Add the marinated lampuki pieces to the soup and allow drawing at a low heat for 5 minutes. Fill the soup into soup-bowls and serve with the bread croutons.

Yellow pepper soup with avocado oil

10 yellow peppers
2 shallots, finely sliced
olive oil for frying
40 ml Noilly Prat
1 sprig thyme
salt, sugar
Tabasco

100 ml avocado oil
1/2 avocado cut in thin slices
1 red pepper, finely sliced – save some of the slices for garnishing
salt & pepper
4 T olive oil
4 baguette slices, cut lengthwise

Remove the pips from the peppers and extract the juice. Using a deep saucepan, lightly fry the shallots in olive oil. Fill in the Noilly Prat with the pepper-juice (apx. 1 litre). Add the sprig of thyme and simmer until the taste of the peppers has developed. Season the soup with salt, a pinch of sugar and a dash of Tabasco, keep the soup warm.

Briefly fry the avocado slices with the red pepper strips in olive oil, season and keep warm. Braise the remaining pepper pieces in olive oil until soft and then puree with a little olive oil. Spread the puree onto the baguette slices and place under the grill or put in the oven until crisp.

Before serving, re-heat the soup and whip in the avocado oil (room temperature) until the mixture becomes frothy. Place the avocado slices and red pepper strips onto hot soup dishes, fill in the soup and »garnish« with a spoonful of avocado oil. Serve with the crisp baguettes.

Artichoke salad with truffles

For servings
4 violet artichokes, cleaned
2 mushrooms
40 g firm summer truffles (from Var region in S. France in June and July)
20 basil leaves, cut into fine strips
olive oil
lemon juice, truffle juice
salt, pepper

Cut the artichokes and mushrooms into very thin slices, and truffles slices must be slightly thicker. Mix with a dressing of basil leaves, olive oil, lemon juice, truffle juice, salt and pepper.

stuffed courgette blossoms in a courgette-mint soup

For 10 portions

10 courgette (zucchini) blossoms
2 shallots, finely chopped
1 green courgette (zucchino), cut up in pieces
1 yellow courgette (zucchino), cut up in pieces
butter for frying
400 g cooked crab or shrimp, cut up in pieces
zest of 1 lime, 1 lemon and 1 orange
1 T basil, finely chopped
1 T tarragon leaves, finely chopped
1 g garlic paste
salt & pepper

For the soup

6 courgettes (about 1 kg)
1 shallots, finely chopped
30 g mint leaves
10 g butter
50 ml olive oil
50 ml mussel stock or white wine

Sauté the shallots and the courgette pieces in butter until soft. Fill into a tureen and stir in the crab (or shrimp) meat, citrus fruit zests, basil, tarragon and the garlic paste. Flavour the mixture with salt and pepper.

Gently fill the mixture inside the courgette blossoms and, shortly before serving, steam the filled blossoms in water favoured with verbena.

Halve the courgette lengthwise, remove the seeds and cut pieces of 2 mm (to look like little half moons). Boil the courgette seeds, one cut-up courgette and the onions in 200 ml water. Simmer for 15 minutes and press the stock through a sieve.

Steam the courgette slices till they are soft, adding the mint leaves towards the end, place the courgettes in iced water and allow draining off. Blend the butter and olive oil at high speed in the mixer. Strain through a sieve and add in enough mussel and vegetable stock to attain the right soup consistency. Briefly stir up with a hand-held mixer.

Fill into soup plates and arrange the stuffed blossoms in the centre.

Coconut soup with tamarillo und crisp peppermint

400 g unsweetened coconut cream (tinned)
50 g refined sugar syrup
300 ml lime
zest of one lime
500 ml Batida de Coco (coconut liqueur)
200 ml tamarind juice
3 small peppermint leaves, finely chopped
1 handful ice cubes
4 thin tamarillo slices
4 deep-fried peppermint leaves
50 g coconut flakes, roasted

Tip For his refined sugar syrup, Rainer Mitze boils one litre of water with 800 g sugar for 8 minutes.

Using an electric mixer, blend together the coconut cream, syrup, lime juice and zest, Batida de Coco, tamarind juice, chopped mint and the ice cubes.

Fill the soup into serving dishes and garnish with the tamarillo slices, fried mint leaves and the coconut flakes.

Creamy, white tomato soup

500 g ripe tomatoes, rinsed and quartered
1 l chicken stock
2 T olive oil
salt & white pepper
2 shallots, finely cubed
2 T olive oil
1 finely chopped garlic clove
100 ml white wine
150 ml cream
50 g butter
3 T whipped cream

Blend the tomato quarters, chicken stock, olive oil, salt and pepper into a fine puree. Fill from the mixer into the saucepan and bring to boil, separate the tomato juice by filling the puree into a cheesecloth, tying a knot and hanging the cloth up.

Stew the shallots and garlic in hot olive oil until they are glazy. Reduce the heat by stirring in the white wine; add the clear tomato juice and leave to simmer.
Add the cream and continue to simmer until the liquid is reduced by 1/3. Work in dabs of cold butter with a hand-held mixer.

Before serving, add the whipped cream and season to taste with salt and white pepper.

Little bonito »hedgehogs« on citrus chutney

600 g bonito (tuna) cut into cubes
zest of 1 lemon
zest of 1 orange
20 g capers, finely chopped
salt
pepper
50 g Kinnie (Maltese bitter lemonade)
2 T olive oil
200 g uncooked spaghetti, roughly ground
200 ml oil for frying

Citrus chutney

150 g sugar
2 T honey liqueur
3 red onions, cut into segments
1/2 tsp red pepper berries
4 blood oranges (juice and segments)
4 lemons (juice and segments)
salt
pepper
4 mint leaves, finely chopped

Mix the tuna with the other ingredients and leave to marinate in the fridge for 1 hour. Coat the tuna with ground spaghetti and fry in hot oil.

Lightly stir-fry the sugar and the honey liqueur till glazy, add the onions and brown them. Pour in the orange and lemon juices and boil down. Add the orange and lemon segments and season to taste.

Fold in the pepper berries and the mint and leave to cool. Serve the bonito hedgehogs with the chutney

Bean-crab salad with calamaretti and beetroot

4 small red beet roots, cooked
300 g Italian white beans, cooked until soft
16 crabs
2 l court bouillon (a Stock prepared by boiling up water and wine with onions, carrots, dill, a bay leaf, parsley sprigs, salt, pepper and pimento seeds)
8 calamaretti (little octopi)
100 ml olive oil
1 garlic clove, pressed
sea salt

For vinaigrette salad dressing

juice of 4 oranges (apx. 200 ml)
1 spice clove
1 mace
1 pinch ginger, freshly grated
1 tsp bitter orange marmalade
2 T olive oil
1 T grape-seed oil
juice of 1/2 lemon
champagne vinegar (a few dashes)
salt & pepper
1 bunch tarragon, finely chopped

Preparing the vinaigrette: Boil up the orange juice with the clove, mace, ginger and marmalade until mixture starts to thicken. Allow to cool before stirring in the olive oil, grape-seed oil, lemon juice and a few dashes of champagne vinegar, season to taste with salt and pepper and add tarragon at end.
Peel beetroot, cut in cubes and marinate with 2 tablespoons of the vinaigrette. Dress the white beans with a little vinaigrette and flavour with salt and pepper if desired.
Boil the crabs in the court bouillon for 2-3 minutes, break off the tails and remove the digestive tracts. Crush the pincers under a saucepan and mix with 2-3 tablespoons of vinaigrette, firmly squeeze out and strain the liquid through a fine sieve. Distribute the liquid over the crab tails.
Skin the calamaretti under running cold water, remove the dark vein on the back and wash the calamaretti thoroughly. Cut the body (but leave the tentacles whole) into thin strips and briefly sauté in hot olive oil with the pressed garlic. Flavour with sea salt, pepper and the orange-vinaigrette.

To serve, place the white beans and crabs in the middle of a plate. Surround with the beetroot cubes and calamaretti. Season with sea salt, pepper and the rest of the vinaigrette.

Orange salad

2 juicy oranges
1 small fennel (150 g)
2 small white onions
1 tsp fresh rosemary
1 T white wine vinegar
4 T olive oil
salt & freshly ground pepper

Peel both oranges, completely removing the white pith and catch the juice in a bowl. Cut the oranges into slices of 1/2 cm, removing the pips. Spread the orange slices out on a large platter.

Clean the fennel and trim off the hard outer parts, reserve the green, feathery leaves for garnishing later. Cut the soft fennel hearts into small cubes and slice the onions into thin rings.

Blend the collected orange juice with white wine vinegar and olive oil. Finely chop the rosemary and stir it into the juice. Season with salt and pepper.

Thoroughly dip the fennel cubes into the sauce and then arrange them on the orange slices. Scatter onion rings over and trickle remaining sauce over the salad.

Bread salad

750 g Maltese white bread which has gone hard
2 large, red onions
4 firm, salad tomatoes
2 stalks celery stalks
1 cucumber
15-20 basil leaves
salt & pepper
1/2 cup olive oil
3-4 T wine vinegar

Tear or cut the bread into small segments and moisten with water. When the bread is thoroughly soaked, squeeze out the excess water and pull the bread into small chunks. Put these into a salad bowl. Cut the onions, tomatoes, celery stalks and peeled cucumber into small pieces. With your fingers, gently pluck off about half of the basil leaves (basil would loose its´ aroma if it where cut with a knife). Season with salt and plenty of freshly ground pepper. Pour olive oil over and store in a cool place for 3–4 hours.
Before serving, fold in the wine vinegar and add the rest of the basil leaves to intensify the aroma. If desired, add more seasoning. Serve cool.

Aubergine puree

800 g aubergines
120 g Tahina (sesame puree)
8 ml lemon juice
40 g fresh garlic, peeled and pressed
salt
40 ml olive oil

40 g pomegranate seeds
mint leaves
pita or flat, unleavened bread

Grill the aubergines till the skins darken and then place them on a baking tray and bake at 220 °C until they are soft. Leave the aubergines to cool overnight. Take the aubergines out of their skins and puree in a mixer. Gradually add in the Tahina and teaspoons of olive oil. Season with lemon juice, garlic and salt.

Bake the pita or flat bread at 220 °C until crisp.

To serve, spoon the aubergine paste into round portions in the centre of the plates. Lightly, in an outward, circular movement, press the tablespoon into the middle. Fill the mould with a spoonful of olive oil. Garnish with pomegranate seeds and mint and serve with crisp, warm bread.

Parsley salad with tomatoes and shrimps

400 g plain-leaved parsley
80 g mint leaves
400 g vine tomatoes
80 g onions
40 g Bulgur (pre-cooked, dried, roughly or finely ground wheat kernels)
80 ml olive oil
50 ml lime juice
salt and pepper

400 g shrimps, cooked and shelled
1 iceberg lettuce or radicchio
100 g Parmesan cheese, freshly grated

Thoroughly rinse the parsley and spin dry. Cut the parsley leaves and the mint leaves into very fine pieces. Skin the tomatoes, remove the pips and cut the flesh into small pieces. Chop up the onions. Mix the parsley, mint, tomatoes, and onions with Bulgur. Pour a dressing of olive oil and lime juice over the salad, then season with salt and pepper.

Spread the lettuce leaves on plates. Arrange the parsley salad on the lettuce leaves and garnish with shrimps, then sprinkle the parmesan over.

stuffed aubergines in saffron pastry on tomato coulis

4 mini aubergines
2 firm, ripe tomatoes
1 courgette
1 T olive oil
1 tsp shallots, finely cubed
salt & freshly ground pepper
40 g mozzarella cheese
1 T croutons
thyme, finely chopped
parsley, finely chopped
30 g pastry dough to make strudel

strudel dough (provides about 150 g)
100 g flour (type 405)
8 g oil
1 g salt
3 T water
oil for brushing over
flour for rolling out
the dough

For the saffron batter
3 T white wine
1 pinch saffron
1 dash olive oil
2 T flour
salt
sugar
oil for deep frying

Preparing the strudel dough: Sift the flour onto working surface and make a hollow in the middle. Add the oil and the salt, and knead into a smooth dough – add the water if necessary. Form into a ball and brush the outside with oil, wrap the dough into clear-wrap foil (this prevents the dough wrinkling or splitting) and place in a cool place for 30 minutes. Spread a cloth out on the working surface; lightly and evenly cover both the cloth and dough ball with flour. Roll out the dough on the cloth - as thinly as possible. Glide the backs of both hands under the rolled out dough, slowly and carefully stretch the dough towards the edge of the table.

Preparing the coulis: Skin and quarter the tomatoes, remove the pips and cut up the flesh. Lay aside 1 tablespoon of tomato pieces for the filling. Fry the tomatoes and shallots in olive oil, and leave to simmer slightly. Cut the courgette into cubes, fry in olive oil and stir in the tomato pieces. Season the coulis with salt and pepper and serve at room temperature.
Halve the aubergines lengthwise and hollow out slightly. For the filling, mix the finely cubed mozzarella with the tomato pieces, croutons, thyme and parsley, season with salt and pepper. Fill this mixture into the aubergine halves, smooth into shape and wrap the aubergines inside the thin layer of strudel dough.

Preparing the saffron batter: Blend the white wine with saffron and olive oil, add the flour and beat into a thick, liquid batter. Season with salt and sugar.
Dip the aubergines in this batter and deep fry at 170 °C for about 4 minutes.
Fill the tomato coulis on plates, arrange the aubergine halves on the coulis and serve.

Red mullet with artichokes, olives and boiled bean puree

2 prickly artichokes
olive oil
4 red mullet fillets, without bones
salt & pepper
20 black, stoned olives
Concassée of a fleshy tomato
140 g Cannellini beans,
pre-soaked in water for 10 hours
4 cherry tomatoes,
baked in the oven for a short time

Remove the artichoke hearts, cut 1 heart in half and fry lightly in olive oil, then cut into small cubes.
Keep the second heart for garnishing later. Shortly before serving, cut the heart into fine slices and fry these in olive oil, allow draining off on a sheet of kitchen paper.

Brush the timbale-moulds with olive oil. Season the fish filets with salt and pepper, then place them in the timbales, filling the centres with the artichoke pieces, black olives and tomato concassée. Trickle the olive oil over the top and bake at 180 °C for 8-10 minutes.

Boil the beans in salted water and drain. In the food-processor, puree the beans with the olive oil (keep a few beans for garnishing later). Season the puree with salt and pepper. Turn the timbales out into the centre of the plates and garnish with olive oil, fried artichokes, olives, beans and baked cherry tomatoes.

Vegetable beignets on a herb coulis

- 100 g carrots, sliced
- 100 g celery, sliced
- 100 g kohlrabi, sliced
- 100 g fine green beans, sliced
- 50 g butter
- 3 dl vegetable bouillon
- 1 pinch sugar
- 1 pinch chopped garlic
- 1 tsp curcuma powder
- 1 pinch powdered ginger
- 2 dl double-thick crème
- 1 egg yolk
- 200 g large spinach leaves
- 1 T flour
- 2 l oil for deep frying

For the batter

- 200 g flour
- 3 T olive oil
- 3 dl beer
- salt, pepper, nutmeg

For the herb coulis

- vegetable stock
- 100 g plain-leaved parsley
- 50 g wild garlic leaves
- 1 dl double-thick crème

Sauté all vegetable pieces in butter, add the vegetable bouillon, sugar, garlic and spices, cover and simmer until cooked.

Strain vegetables through a sieve; keep some of the stock for the herb sauce. Boil down the rest of the stock until it has a syrupy consistency. Remove from heat and beat in the egg yolk. Return the vegetables to the soup and allow to cool over several hours.

Blanch the spinach leaves and dry-off well, place vegetable mixture in centre of the leaves and wrap inside. Lightly coat in flour.

Prepare the batter by stirring the ingredients together. Dip the stuffed spinach leaves into the batter and deep-fry in the oil at 180 °C until crisp.

Boil up the reserved vegetable stock; add the rinsed parsley and the wild garlic leaves. Blend in the double-thick crème and season.

Fill the coulis onto plates, and place the beignets on top.

spinach leaves in a honey crust

500 G SPINACH LEAVES
2 EGGS
50 G HONEY
1 TSP LEMON JUICE
25 G STARCH-FLOUR
50 G FLOUR
250 ML PEANUT OIL
COARSE-GRAINED SALT

Remove the stalks from the spinach leaves and rinse several times in fresh water. Allow to drain in a colander, and then dry on a cloth or a sheet of kitchen paper.

Boil 4 l of water with a handful of coarse-grained salt. Prepare a large bowl of iced water.

Briefly add the spinach leaves to the boiling water. Remove the leaves with a skimming ladle and cool-off very briefly in the iced water, then empty into the colander to drain. Make sure this blanching process doesn't damage the leaves Once more, dry the leaves on a cloth or a sheet of kitchen paper.

Beat the eggs well. Now prepare a large frying pan.

Pour in the oil and heat it up at a medium setting. Wrap 3 or 4 spinach leaves together into flat parcels. Coat the parcels with flour and the beaten eggs before putting them into the pan.

Gently turn them with the skimming ladle, making sure they don't get damaged. Remove the parcels from pan and lay them on a sheet of kitchen paper.

Blend warmed-up honey with the lemon juice and brush this mixture onto the spinach parcels, immediately sift starch flour onto them, so that a crispy crust develops.

These crispy spinach parcels can be served with olive oil mixed with honey and lemon juice or a chickpea paste with pine nuts.

Baked and chilled tomato terrine

10 ripe red tomatoes
salt, pepper, sugar
thyme, finely chopped
rosemary, finely chopped
garlic cloves, finely sliced
olive oil
3 1/2 sheets gelatine; soak and remove excess water
1/4 l tomato consommé

Blanch the tomatoes, peel, and quarter and remove the pips. Place on a baking tray and season with salt and pepper.
Sprinkle thyme and rosemary over the tomatoes, then spread the garlic slices over the top and trickle with olive oil. Bake in the oven at 80 °C for apx. 3 hours. Thereafter allow to drain-off on a cloth.

Dissolve the soaked and well wrung out gelatine sheets in the tomato consommé. Place a terrine on a bed of ice, and alternately filling in layers of the tomatoes and the gelatinised consommé.

Place the terrine in the fridge until firm and then slice with an electric knife.

Mushrooms au gratin

250 g spinach leaves
25 g butter
salt & freshly ground pepper
250 g champignon mushrooms
250 g oyster mushrooms
2 shallots, finely chopped
30 g butter
4 egg yolks
2 T white wine
2 T mushroom stock

For the sauce
100 ml mushroom stock
100 ml truffle juice
80 g butter
salt & freshly ground pepper

Blanche the cleaned and rinsed spinach leaves, briefly immerse in iced water and allow to drain. Lightly sauté the leaves in melted butter and season. Gently brown the mushrooms and the shallots in butter and season. Place the spinach into 4 cylinder-shaped oven dishes (diameter: 7 cm) and spread the fried mushrooms on top.

Preheat the oven to 160 °C. Whip the egg yolk, the white wine and the mushroom stock into an airy zabaglione and fill into the dishes. Place these into the preheated oven for 12 minutes.

For the sauce: simmer the mushroom stock and truffle juice down, till it has a thicker consistency. Add the in cold butter and puree, seasoning with salt and freshly ground pepper.

Remove the baked mushroom gratins from their dishes and place on warm plates before pouring the sauce over top.

seafood salad

500 g squid
100 g prawns, cooked & peeled
2 lemons
1 bunch plain-leaved parsley
1 tsp fresh oregano
1-2 red, pickled pepperonis
2 garlic cloves
5 T high quality olive oil
salt, freshly ground pepper

Preparing the squid: Thoroughly rinse the squid under running water and remove the thin skin. Turn the head and the innards inside out, and remove these.

Boil up 1 l water, the juice of 1/2 a lemon and 1/2 tsp. of salt in a saucepan. Add the cleaned squid, cover and allow too simmer for about 30 minutes until tender (test with a skewer). Pour off the water and allow the squid to drain. Cut the tentacles into pieces and the squid outside into fine rings. Mix with the prawns in a bowl.

For the marinade: Remove the pips from the pepperonis and cut them into fine rings, and finely chop 2 garlic cloves. Blend 2-3 T of lemon juice with 5 T of olive oil. Stir in the pepperoni rings and garlic, then season with salt, pepper and oregano.

Pour the marinade over the squid and prawns, and mix together well. Chill in the fridge for at least 2 hours, allowing the salad to draw.

Approximately 15 minutes before serving, take the salad out of the fridge. Finely chop the parsley and fold in. Once more, season with salt and pepper, and if desired, a little lemon juice. Garnish the salad with lemon slices.

Lukewarm fish salad with silver beet and dandelion leaves

12 small red mullets
1 dlolive oil
juice of 1 lemon
silver beet
1 fennel
olive oil
100 wild dandelion leaves, cleaned
sea salt
pepper
1 T basil in olive oil

Carefully fillet the red mullets and lay them in an ovenproof dish. Brush the fish with olive oil and bake at 220 °C for 4–5 minutes. Remove the filets from the oven and cool off the fish stock by adding lemon juice, then set aside. Later, before serving, reheat the stock and stir in the remaining lemon juice and olive oil to make a sauce.

Blanch the silver beet leaves, chill-off in iced water and drain on kitchen roll paper. Cut the fennel into thin slices, lightly salt and cook slowly in olive oil at a low setting.

Spread the silver beet and the dandelion leaves on the plates, pour the sauce over and season with a pinch of sea salt and freshly ground pepper. In the middle, place the fennel slices and arrange the fish around the fennel. Flavour with a little basil in olive oil.

Rosemary and olive oil jelly with potato slices and onion sauce

1 large potato for slicing, peeled
3 large potatoes that stay firm when boiled
sea salt
balsamic vinegar
2 dl extra vergine olive oil
2 beetroots
1 Spanish onion
1 dl cream
2 dl poultry stock
2 T whipped cream
salt, pepper
1 sprig rosemary
2 sheets gelatine

Peel the potatoes and cut them into cubes, boil the cubes in sea saltwater until »al dente«.

For the crisps: use a bread-slicing machine to cut the potato into 8 thin slices. Add a drop of balsamic vinegar onto 4 of the slices and cover these with those remaining. Shortly before serving, deep-fry the slices in half of the olive oil and then to drain them on kitchen paper.

Cook and peel the beetroots, put 2 of them in the juice extractor. Straining the juice through a fine sieve and then boil the liquid till it has a syrup-like consistency. Cut the onion into chunks and cook until soft in the poultry stock with cream. Puree in the mixer, blend in the whipped cream, season and mix again.

Heat the remaining olive oil with the rosemary sprig, then leave to draw. Dissolve the soaked and pressed-out sheet of gelatine in the oil and fold in with the whisk. Pour to a flat dish with a depth of about 5 millimetres and chill in the freezer to solidify. Cut the jelly into cubes just before serving.

Pour 1 or 2 drops of balsamic vinegar on the fried potato cubes, pour in the frothy onion sauce and arrange on the plates, surround with potato fritters, beetroot crisps and olive oil jelly. Garnish with the balsamic vinegar, onion sauce and beetroot syrup.

Fried potatoes with olive crème

100 g black olives without stones
1 T capers
1 T pine nuts
2 tsp tomato puree

4 T olive oil
1 tsp aceto balsamico (herb vinegar)
white pepper, freshly ground
4 lengthy, flattish potatoe

Using a (hand) mixer, blend the olives, capers, pine nuts and tomato puree with 2 T of oil. Season the crème with aceto balsamico and pepper.

Peel potatoes (young potatoes can be left unpeeled) and halve lengthwise. Heat the remaining oil in a frying pan, add the potatoes and and fry at medium setting for about 7 minutes with the lid on. Turn the potatoes and fry without the lid for another 7 minutes, until potatoes are soft and golden-brown.

If necessary, salt the potatoes, then spread on the olive crème and serve hot.

Spinach rolls with lampuki in lime vinaigrette

200 g lampuki (sea bream),
without skin and bones
4 T olive oil
1 T lime juice
1 tsp Pommery mustard
salt & freshly ground pepper
20 young spinach leaves, rinsed and dried
2 limes, cut the skins into fine strips
1 thick carrot,
peeled and cut into thin strips
1 T lime juice
2 T olive oil
salt

Cut the fish filets into very thin slices.

Mix the oil, lime juice, mustard, salt and freshly ground pepper. Coat the fish slices in this mixture.

Wrap a spinach leaf around each fish slice.

Prepare a marinade of lime juice, olive oil and salt.

Arrange the spinach-fish rolls on plates and garnish with the carrots and lime strips then trickle the marinade thereon. Season again with salt and freshly ground pepper.

White tomato-mousse on marinated tomatoes

10-15 TOMATOES
SALT, CAYENNE PEPPER, SUGAR
10 GIN
1/4 LEMON, THE JUICE THEREOF
10 G CHAMPAGNE VINEGAR
6 G ELATINE SHEETS, SOAKED IN COLD WATER AND SQUEEZED OUT
150 G WHIPPED CREAM

Preparing the mousse: Chop the tomatoes into small pieces, then season with salt, pepper and sugar. Add the gin, lemon juice and vinegar and blend into a fine puree. Pour the puree into cheesecloth and close it with a knot. Hang the cloth up overnight to drain into a bowl. Depending on the type of tomatoes used, this should provide about 1/2 a litre of juice.

Season the juice and slightly warm it up and dissolve the gelatine therein. Place the bowl on ice and whisk until it becomes foamy and light. Just before the mixture goes solid, fold in the cream (which must not be too stiffly whipped). Quickly transfer the mousse into an icing bag and decoratively squeeze into the dishes and cool in the fridge for an hour.

FOR THE MARINATED TOMATOES
2 T CHAMPAGNE VINEGAR
SOME LEMON JUICE
6 T TOMATO CONSOMMÉ
1 SMALL SHALLOT, CHOPPED AND BLANCHED
SALT, PEPPER, SUGAR
6 T OLIVE OIL
5 BASIL LEAVES
8 TOMATOES

Preparing the marinade: stir the champagne vinegar, lemon juice, tomato consommé and chopped shallots together and season with salt, pepper and a pinch of sugar. Stir in the olive oil and the basil leaves. Allow the taste develop for 1/2 an hour.

Blanch the tomatoes, skin and cut in thin slices. Season with salt, pepper and a pinch of sugar. Pour the marinade over the tomato slices and allow too draw for 1 – 2 hours.

Lay the tomato slices onto plates, trickle some marinade over and arrange the mousse on top

Potato waffles with goat's cheese sauce and Parma ham

For the waffles

500 g potatoes, boiled and mashed
100 g cream
6 egg yolks
4 eggs
50 g sifted flour
50 g soft butter
2 T chopped parsley
salt, white pepper & nutmeg

Goat´s cheese sauce

450 g goat´s cheese
salt
white pepper, freshly ground
lemon juice
1 tsp aniseed liqueur
150 g whipped cream
3 sheets gelatine,
soaked and dissolved

For the waffles: Whisk the ingredients into a smooth batter, cover and leave to stand for about 15 minutes. Lightly butter the waffle iron and fill in a ladle of the potato batter. Bake until golden yellow.

Briefly warm up the goat´s cheese and then season it with salt, pepper, lemon juice and aniseed liqueur. Stir in the dissolved gelatine and allow cooling for a short time. Fold in the whipped cream and chill.

Serve the waffles and the cheese with Parma ham. An excellent accompaniment to Parma ham would be deep fried spring leeks.

spinach toast with manchego cheese

For the spinach toasts
4 slices white bread (each 20 g)
800 g fresh spinach
4 T olive oil
salt
freshly ground pepper
freshly grated nutmeg
10 g roasted almond splitters

1 T olive oil
4 slices cooked ham

For the cheese sauce
70 g butter
20 g flour
200 ml milk
100 g cream
salt
freshly ground pepper
freshly grated nutmeg
4 egg yolks
40 g freshly grated
matured Manchego cheese

Remove the stems from the spinach leaves and blanch in boiling, salted water until the leaves soften. Remove and allow the leaves to drain, lightly press to extract excess water.

Heat the oil in a large casserole and stir-fry the spinach for 4–6 minutes. Season with salt, pepper and nutmeg, then fold the almond splinters under.

For the cheese sauce: Gently melt 20 g butter in a heavy-based saucepan. Add the flower and blend into the butter to make a smooth roux. Stir constantly for 2–3 minutes (do not let the mixture turn brown). Gradually pour in the milk and cream, bring to boil while stirring constantly thus allowing the sauce to thicken. Season with salt, pepper and nutmeg. Remove from heat and set aside.
Beat together the remaining butter with the egg yolks until creamy. Gently, together with the cheese, fold into the sauce.

Lightly toast the slices of bread and lay them on a baking tray. Briefly fry the slices of ham in olive oil, then place the ham onto the bread slices. Lay the spinach over ham and cover with the cheese sauce.
Grill in a pre-heated oven at 200 °C to gratiné. When the cheese is golden and bubbling, remove from the oven and serve immediately.

Artichokes with mussel sauce

8 violet-coloured artichokes
1 T olive oil
1 T lemon juice
1/2 glass water
salt & pepper
12 mussels
12 cockles
12 clams
3-4 T young broad beans, removed from pods
4 slices Parmesan cheese

Clean the artichokes. Heat up the olive oil, lemon juice and water in a steamer or fish kettle; add the artichokes and season with salt and pepper. Cover the pot with aluminium foil and cook for 5 minutes at medium heat.

After about 2/3 of the cooking time, add the cleaned shellfish. They will then open their shells, thus adding their liquid to the sauce.

Remove the artichokes and keep them warm. Strain the stock through a very fine sieve or cloth, boil the resultant liquid until it has been reduced to a volume of about 8 tablespoons. The seafood is no longer needed and should be stored and used for another recipe.

Arrange the artichokes and the broad beans garnish with spoonfuls of sauce. Season with freshly ground pepper and a few drops of olive oil and decorate the artichokes with the Parmesan cheese.

Vegetable carpaccio with olive vinaigrette

8 white asparagus spears
8 green asparagus spears
(may be substituted by another Maltese vegetable)
1 cauliflower
2 T carrots, cubed
1/3 leek
salt

For the vinaigrette
1 T olive puree (tapenade)
1–2 T olive oil
1/2 tsp sherry vinegar
1/2 tsp balsamico vinegar
salt & freshly ground pepper

Peel the asparagus and cut off the ends. Cut 4 firm, decorative florets out of the cauliflower. Boil the vegetables in slightly salted water until cooked »al dente« and then shock-off the vegetables in iced water.

Briefly blanch the carrot pieces and cut the leek in 4 slices. At a low heat allow the vegetables to simmer in a tightly-sealed casserole. Once cooked, allow the vegetables to cool. Using a slicing-machine, cut the cooked vegetables evenly into thin slices and arrange on plates with a leek slice in the centre.

Prepare the vinaigrette by blending the ingredients together and season to taste. Before serving, trickle the vinaigrette over the vegetable slices and decorate with carrot pieces.

Fried vegetables on a savoury sabayon

200 g broccoli florets
200 g cauliflower florets
200 g courgettes (zucchini)
200 g aubergines
2 tomatoes
salt, pepper, flour
peanut oil for deep frying

For the batter
200 g flour
3 T olive oil
3 dl beer
salt & freshly ground pepper
nutmeg, freshly grated

For the savoury sabayon
3 egg yolks
30 g caper vinegar
2 T double cream
1 dl vegetable broth
salt, pepper & cayenne
sea salt

Strongly season the prepared vegetables with salt and freshly ground pepper, lightly coat the vegetables with flour and dip them into in the batter. Deep-fry the vegetable pieces in the peanut oil (180 °C) until they are golden brown.

Preparing the sabayon: Whip the egg yolks and the caper vinegar together over hot water (perhaps using a bain-marie) until the mixture is light and airy. Gradually add the double cream and then the vegetable broth.

Fold in the caper juice and season sabayon with salt, pepper and cayenne. Arrange the fried vegetables on the sabayon and serve with sea salt.

Veal carpaccio served with olive sauce and pine nuts

For 6 servings

500 g veal filet
60 g pine nuts, roasted
30 chervil leaves

For the olive sauce
6 cl strong broth
3 T aceto balsamico (Italian balm vinegar)
1 tsp sherry vinegar
90 g olive caviar (black olives pickled in olive oil, then pureed)
4 T olive oil
salt
pepper, freshly ground

Firmly roll the veal filet in transparent foil and place it in the freezer. Cut the frozen filet into extremely thin slices and place the slices on cold plates.

Place the ingredients for the olive sauce in a bowl and stir together well. Flavour to taste.

Brush a thin layer of the sauce onto the filet slices, garnish with a scattering of pine nuts and top with chervil leaves. The dish is now ready to be served.

squid salad with mint

500 g squid
salt
1 large tomato
2 small red onions
1 red chilli pepper
1 green chilli pepper
20 g mint
3 T lemon juice
sea salt, pepper

Skin the squid and pull the tentacles out of the bag-like body. Remove of the innards. Rinse the body and the tentacles well.

Cut body into strips and boil it in salted water with the tentacles, the meat should not get too soft.

To remove the tomato skins, make a cross-shaped slit on the top and scald by boiling water over the tomato, thereafter immerse in cold water and peel the skin off. Remove the pips and cut the tomato into strips.

Peel the onions, halve the chilli and remove the pips. Cut these into strips.

Rinse the mint and cut it into strips. Mix the ingredients with the squid and seasoning to taste with lemon juice, sea salt and pepper.

MAIN COURSE DISHES

Fish, Meat

Vegetables, Pasta

Dips, Chutneys

Gourmet pastries with tomatoes and basil

3 kg large tomatoes
3 green, thick-fleshed peppers
1 large onion
4 peeled garlic cloves
1 bouquet of various kitchen herbs
4 green thyme sprigs, with the leaves removed
2 T tomato paste
salt & freshly ground pepper
20 g powdered sugar
150 g butter
1 dl olive oil
4 phyllo pastry (can be purchased ready-made from Asian food shops)
2 T fresh basil, chopped

Skin the tomatoes by scalding them in boiling water and then immersing them in iced water. Peel, cut into quarters and remove the pips. With a tomato cutter (1 inch = 2.5 cm wide) cut discs out of the tomato flesh. Cut the remainders of the tomatoes into small pieces.

Rinse the green peppers and carefully remove the white areas and pips. Cut the peppers into 3 (lengthwise) and then, using the tomato cutter, cut out discs. Blanche the discs in boiling water for 10 seconds, then plunge into iced water and allow to drain.

Peel the onions and chop these finely. Stir-fry the onions in 25 g of butter, 50 ml of olive oil and a little salt for 3 - 4 minutes at medium heat (the onions shouldn't go brown). Add the garlic cloves, the herb-bouquet, thyme, tomato pieces and tomato paste, then season with salt, pepper and powdered sugar. Allow to simmer at medium heat in an open pot until the liquid has evaporated. Remove the garlic cloves and the herbs from the tomato sauce.

Cut out 4 circles of greaseproof paper (about 13 cm diameter) and cut 20 pastry circles to fit. Lay a pastry circle onto a baking tray and brush with butter, then place another circle on top and again brush with butter till you have a pile of 5 circles. The fifth circle is not buttered. Make another 3 piles of pastry circles. Place the 4 pastries in the fridge.

Melt the remaining butter and lightly fry the tomato and paprika discs. Place these discs on the 4 greaseproof paper circles; work in rounds, overlapping the edges (creating an appearance of roof tiles). Cool in the fridge so that the butter can solidify thus keeping the discs on the greaseproof paper.

Bake the pastry piles for 10 minutes at 200 °C until the dough is lightly browned.
Gently heat up the tomato sauce, season and fold in the fresh basil. Spread this mixture over the pastries.
Turn the well-cooled tomato and paprika slices onto the pastries (the greaseproof paper must now be on top) and bake in the oven at 200 °C for 8 minutes.

Before serving, remove greaseproof paper and flavour with salt, pepper, thyme and a little olive oil.

Braised rabbit with fennel

1.2 kg rabbit – oven-ready (preferably including the liver)
50 g uncooked ham-slices
50 g salami slices
50 g streaky bacon slices
2 fennels (500 g)
1/2 untreated lemon
4 garlic cloves
1 tsp fresh rosemary
1 day old bread rolls (without the crust)
1/4 l dry white wine
125 g cream
6 T olive oil
6 peppercorns
salt & freshly ground pepper

Rinse the rabbit and dry well. Rub salt and pepper into the meat – inside and outside. Keep the liver for the stuffing. Cube the bread roll and soak in 125 ml of white wine.

Clean the fennel and trim off the stalks, put aside the green, feathery leaves for later. Heat 750 ml of salted water. Cut the lemon into slices, peel 2 garlic cloves and add to the water with the peppercorns. Cook the fennel bulbs with the stalks for about 15 minutes, and then remove. Strain the broth through a sieve and put aside. Cover the fennel bulbs to use later. Finely chop the fennel stalks and 1/2 of the fennel greenery.

Cut the ham and salami into tiny cubes. Chop the rabbit liver into small pieces, mince the 2 garlic cloves, and the rosemary. Gently squeeze-out the bread cubes. Mix the above with the chopped fennel and season the filling with salt and freshly ground pepper.

Pre-heat the oven to 175 °C. Stuff the rabbit with the filling and sew up the opening with kitchen thread. Heat the olive oil in a flameproof casserole with a tight-fitting lid; briefly brown the stuffed rabbit on all sides.

Pour 1/2 of the fennel stock over the rabbit, cover and braise in the oven for about an hour. Occasionally turn the rabbit and trickle fennel broth over, add more fennel broth if necessary.

Approximately 10 minutes before end of the braising time, finely slice the fennel bulb and cut the bacon into small pieces. Fry the bacon in order to draw out the fat and remove any crisp pieces. Gently fry the fennel slices in the bacon fat, adding a few tablespoons of fennel stock. Flavour with salt and freshly ground pepper.

Remove the rabbit from the flameproof casserole and keep it warm in the oven. Add 125ml of wine and 125 g cream to the stock then boil down on at a high setting. Cut the meat into slices and arrange on plate with the fennel. Chop the remaining fennel greenery and scatter it and the bacon crisps over the rabbit before serving.

Orange-flavoured rabbit filets on ratatouille

8 rabbit filets without skin and sinews
salt & black pepper
Maltese olive oil
2 T butter
zest of 2 oranges
zest of 1 lemon
6 slices white toast bread, without crust, ground to breadcrumbs
1 tsp chopped rosemary
1/2 tsp chopped garlic
1 T finely chopped plain-leaved parsley

250 g yellow-green courgette, finely diced
100 g onions, cut into small pieces
250 g red and yellow peppers, cut into small cubes
6 garlic cloves, finely chopped
Maltese olive oil
butter
salt & pepper
caraway seeds
garam marsala (blend of Indian spices)
1 hot chilli pepper
50 g fresh Parmesan cheese, grated

Season the rabbit filets and briefly fry in olive oil, then lie on a grid and allow to cool slightly.

Mix the breadcrumbs with the orange, lemon, garlic, rosemary and parsley and coat the rabbit filets in this mixture. Lightly press the breadcrumb layer into place and fry in olive oil and butter.

Warm up olive oil and butter and brown the onions and garlic, then add the caraway seeds and garam marsala. Lightly brown the courgettes (zucchinis), peppers and the chilli peppers. Allow the above ingredients to simmer for 5 minutes and season.

Place the ratatouille vegetables in the centre of the plate and lay the rabbit filets on top before scattering with Parmesan cheese.

Rabbit fillets served with polenta and cotechino sauce

400 g rabbit saddle, boned
4 streaky bacon slices
150 g rabbit innards (liver, heart, kidneys)
2 shallots, finely chopped
extra vergine olive oil
1/2 glass Lambrusco (Italian red wine)
1/2 l brown rabbit stock
80 g large spinach leaves
salt
150 g maize flour (for the polenta)
rosemary essence (press fresh rosemary through a juice extractor)
1 piece of bacon rind
150 g cotechino
(a large, spicy pork sausage)
white wine
1/2 white onion, chopped

Cover the rabbit saddle with bacon slices and truss with kitchen thread. Steam for apx. 4 minutes in a steamer (or braise in a copper pan), then remove the meat and keep it warm.

Clean and cube the innards. Lightly fry the shallots, add the innards and cool down with some of the Lambrusco. Boil down a little and add some rabbit stock, allow to simmer briefly before seasoning.

Blanch the spinach leaves in salted water, immerse in iced water and allow draining. Line 4 dishes with spinach (these only serve as moulds to shape the leaf »parcels«). Arrange innards on the spinach cover these with leaves and keep warm.

With 100 g maize flour make a polenta in the usual way and flavour with a few drops of rosemary essence and extra-vergine olive oil. Roll out the polenta and cut out 4 circles, fry these in a thick-based pan which has been greased with bacon rind until they are crisp on the outside.

For the sauce: boil the cotechino in water with a dash of white wine for about an hour and a half, and then roughly chop up the sausage. Keep 2 thin slices for garnishing later.

Stir-fry the onion in oil until it is a pale yellow colour, add the cotechino to the pan and fry it till browned. Pour in the remaining Lambrusco and boil down. Fill in the rabbit stock and boil for 5-6 minutes, then season to taste. Puree the cotechino sauce in a blender, then using a hand-held mixer beat until light and creamy before serving.

Roast the remaining maize flour in a heavy cast-iron pan. Brown the rabbit meat and coat in the roasted maize flour, return to the pan and fry until the outside is crispy.

Open the saddle by cutting along the middle, then serve with the sauce and the stuffed spinach leaves and the polenta, each of these decorated with 1/2 a cotechino slice.

Leg of rabbit in olive oil with mild garlic and potatoes

4 RABBIT HAUNCHES (LEGS)
100 G FINE SEA SALT
4 SPRIGS OF ROSEMARY
GREEN PEPPER, FRESHLY GROUND
12 GARLIC CLOVES
4 DL OLIVE OIL
28 SMALL, YOUNG POTATOES
1 ROMANESCO BROCCOLI
1 FIRM TOMATO
BALSAMICO VINEGAR

Rub the sea salt and pepper onto the rabbit legs and leave to stand for 1 1/2 hours. Heat the olive oil in a metal roasting pan, add the legs, rosemary and peeled garlic cloves and allow the flavour to develop at 95 °C for apx. 45 minutes. Occasionally (using an uncooked spaghetti noodle) check if the meat is tender and the haunches are cooked. Remove the legs and the garlic from the roasting pan and keep warm.

Separately, blanch the potatoes and romanesco florets. Simmer the potatoes in the frying oil left over from the rabbit legs for about 10 minutes.

Skin the tomatoes and remove the pips, cut the flesh into fine strips and briefly fry in olive oil.

To serve, lay out rabbit haunches and the garlic, and then arrange the potatoes and romanesco florets. Finally place the tomato strips on the meat and scatter with sea salt. Mix the olive oil with some balsamico vinegar and serve with the braised rabbit.

smoked rabbit on pea cream with a »pepper-cheese lasagne«

4 rabbit saddles (backs)
salt & pepper
lemon-thyme
oil for frying
2 yellow peppers
2 red peppers
400 g fresh peas
100 g poultry stock
salt, pepper
lemon peel finely cut up

For the cheese mousse
200 g fresh goat´s cheese
200 g Rondin de chèvre
(a soft French goat´s cheese
with a mouldy rind)
30 g poultry stock
1/2 sheet gelatine
70 g whipping cream
salt & cayenne pepper

Flavour the saddles with salt and pepper, briefly brown all sides in a little oil and lemon-thyme. Cure the meat in a smoking oven for about 3-4 minutes (do not smoke too strongly).

Bake the peppers at 200 °C in a hot oven for 20-30 minutes, thereafter skin the peppers and cut into large, even rectangles and then season.

For the sauce: blanch the peas, immerse in iced water and drain off. Puree the peas with poultry stock and lemon-thyme by pushing though a fine sieve, then season with salt and pepper.

For the cheese mousse: put the 2 goat´s cheeses and 1/2 of the poultry stock into the blender, puree then flavour with salt and pepper. Soak the gelatine in cold water and then press out the water, dissolve the gelatine in the remaining poultry stock and add to the cheese. Fold in the whipped cream, then pour the mouse into small terrine and allow too cool for 2-3 hours.

To serve, cut the mousse into slices and arrange the pepper rectangles and the cheese mousse in layers (like a pasta lasagne)
Place the smoked, lukewarm rabbit on the cold pea cream and serve with the pepper-cheese mousse lasagne.

Braised shoulder of lamb with a lemon-caper sauce

For the stock

500 g lamb bones
2 l water
1 sprig thyme
4 bay leaves
1 bunch stock vegetables
(e.g. onion, carrot, celery bulb,
parsley, etc.)
2 garlic cloves
10 pepper corns
parsley
salt

For the shoulder of lamb

1.5 kg boned lamb shoulder
2 T chopped garlic
1 sprig rosemary
salt, pepper
2 T oil
100 g roughly cut up shallots
zest of 1 lemon
4 unpeeled garlic cloves

For the sauce

50 g butter
30 g shallots, finely chopped
2 T lemon juice
200 g lamb fond from the bottom
of roasting tin
corn-flour, for thickening
1 dl cream

For the stuffing

2 T capers
segments of 2 lemons
1 T chopped parsley
1 T whipped cream

Make a lamb stock by boiling up the ingredients listed above for about 3 hours, then strain through a sieve.

Spread out the shoulder, season and sprinkle with garlic and rosemary needles. Roll up the meat and truss (bind) it with kitchen thread. Heat the oil in a flameproof casserole or roasting tin and lightly fry the shallots, garlic and lemon zest, add the meat-roll and brown on all sides. Add the lambstock and put the casserole in the oven to roast for about 1 hour at 180 °C until the lamb is tender. Remove thread and keep the meat warm.

For the sauce: brown the shallots in butter and pour lemon juice and lamb stock into the pan. Add the cream and boil down, if thickening is required, stir in some corn-flour. Season the sauce with salt and pepper, and then fold in the stuffing and the whipped cream.

Carve the shoulder of lamb and serve with the sauce and vegetables of choice.

Barbecued lamb chops

Wash and peel the apple, remove the core und cut into small pieces. Peel the onion and cut into little cubes.

Heat the olive oil in a saucepan and lightly fry the onion pieces, fold in the apple pieces, mustard, ketchup, sugar, orange and lemon juice. Allow to simmer at a low heat for apx. 10 minutes, stirring occasionally. Season with salt, pepper and oregano.

Pre-heat the grill. Rinse the lamb chops under cold water and dab dry with kitchen roll paper. Flavour with salt and pepper. Briefly pre-grill both sides, then brush on the sauce and return to the grill.

Ingredients for 6 servings

1 sour cooking apple
1 onion
2 T olive oil
2 T hot mustard
4 T tomato ketchup
2 T sugar
juice of 2 lemons
juice of 2 oranges
salt & freshly ground pepper
1 tsp dried oregano
12 lamb chops

Leg of lamb roasted with garlic

Pre-heat the oven to 200 °C. Rinse leg of lamb and dab dry then rub-in olive oil, salt and pepper. Place in a roasting pan. Peel the onion and the garlic and then cut into segments. Add the onion, garlic, marjoram and the bay leaves into the roaster with the lamb. Pour over 250 ml of wine or broth and place the lamb on the lowest shelf in the oven.

Leave the leg of lamb to roast at 200 °C (convectional oven) for about 1 1/4 hours. In between baste the lamb with the juices given of and also pour the rest of the wine over, bit by bit. Remove the lamb from the roaster and keep it warm. Pick out the bay leaves and marjoram. Stir the olives into the gravy and place the roaster onto the stove and allow to gravy boil briefly. Season the sauce.

Serve the leg of lamb with the garlic sauce.

1 small leg of lamb (about 1.4 kg)
2 T cold pressed olive oil,
salt
pepper, freshly ground
1 large onion
8–10 large fresh garlic cloves
6 sprigs marjoram
4 bay leaves
750 ml dry white wine or vegetable broth
125 g green olives
125 g black olives

Marinated fennel with saffron and fried langoustines

For 4–6 servings

2 fennel bulbs
1/2 l tomato consommé
2 shallots, finely chopped
1 garlic clove, pressed
1 pinch saffron threads
salt, pepper, lemon
champagne vinegar,
cayenne pepper
100 ml vegetable oil
100 g mange-tout peas
(peas in the pod)
sugar
16 langoustines
salt, lemon
thin fennel slices, blanched
50 g flour
50 g maizena (corn starch)
3 T white wine
2 T olive oil
salt, cayenne pepper
3 T iced water
oil for frying

Cut the fennel bulbs into thin slices of 2 mm. Boil up the tomato consommé with the shallots, garlic and saffron. Season with salt, pepper and lemon juice and simmer for apx. 10 minutes.
Remove the marinade from the stove; add the fennel slices and a blend of champagne vinegar with olive oil – strongly flavoured with salt and cayenne pepper. Leave to draw for at least 3 hours (or over night).
Briefly fry the mange-tout peas in a little hot oil, season with salt and a pinch of sugar and dress the peas with a spoonful of the fennel marinade.

Open the langoustines and remove the digestive tracts then season with salt and lemon, wrap a fennel slice around each one and fasten with a toothpick. Make a batter consisting of flour, maizena, white wine, oil, salt, cayenne pepper and iced water. Allow to stand for 30 minutes.

Dip the langoustines in the batter and fry in hot oil until golden brown then allow the excess oil to drip off onto kitchen paper. Serve the langoustines with the marinated fennel and the mange-tout peas.

Spicy fish and vegetable kebabs

900 g monkfish or lampuki (sea bream) without the head
250 ml water
6 T lemon juice

For the sauce
4 red chilli peppers, without pips and finely chopped
olive oil
2 large tomatoes, skinned and cut into small pieces
1 sprig oregano
1 tsp freshly ground pepper
1 tsp caraway seeds
1 tsp ground ginger
2 tsp chopped garlic
550 ml fish stock
1/2 large cucumber
1 medium-sized red onion
lime slices

Skin the fish and remove the bones, then cut the fish into large cubes. Marinate the fish for at least 4 hours (or even better, overnight) in a mix of water and lemon juice.

Briskly darken the chillies by frying in olive oil. Add the chopped tomatoes, oregano, ground pepper, caraway seeds, ginger, and garlic and fish stock to the pot and bring to boil. Simmer for 10 minutes more before removing from heat.

Cut cucumber into slices of about 1/2 cm thick and the red onion into 8 (lengthwise). Thread the onion pieces, fish cubes and the cucumber slices alternately on to wooden kebab skewers until only the ends are free.

Generously cover the skewers with sauce and serve with lime slices.

Cod with pastis, thyme and fennel

500 g cod, skinned and filleted
olive oil, salt, pepper

250 g young fennel, finely chopped
30 g shallots cut into cubes
50 ml olive oil
50 ml Pastis (anise-based liqueur)
1 sprig of thyme
1 garlic clove, pressed and in it's skin
2 star-anis, pounded by pestle and mortar
2 pinches orange zest
2 pinches saffron threads
lemon juice
100 ml white wine
50 ml Noilly Prat (bitter liqueur)
500 ml strong fish stock
50 g butter

For the vegetables
3 sprigs of thyme
100 g seaweed
2 small peppers
olive oil, thyme
1 pinch garlic powder
2 small fennels with greenery
4 small courgettes (zucchini)

Cut the fish filets into slices of 5mm. Trickle olive oil onto 4 plates and sprinkle with salt and pepper. Arrange the fish on the plates in a circular forms and season with salt and pepper. Cover the plates with transparent foil and cook in a pre-heated oven at 85 °C for 8-10 minutes.

Preparing the pastis stock: Blend the fennel and the shallots with olive oil, add the pastis, thyme, garlic, star-anis, orange zest, saffron, lemon juice, salt and pepper. Cover and marinate for at least 2 hours. Sauté the ingredients, pour in the white wine and the Noilly Prat. Add the fish stock and leave to draw at a low heat for an hour. When the fennel is soft, pour off the stock and reduce to apx. 300 ml before blending in butter and a dash of pastis.

Preparing the vegetables: first make the thyme powder by drying the thyme sprigs in the microwave oven for 3 minutes then finely cutting up the green leaves.
Blanch the seaweed. Halve the peppers and trickle with olive oil. Add thyme and garlic then season with salt and pepper. Bake the peppers at 100 °C for 20 minutes and remove the skins. Peel the fennel and finely chop the greenery. Cut the courgettes and the fennel into thin slices and fry these in olive oil, flavouring with salt, thyme powder and 4 T pastis stock. Fold in the seaweed and paprika.

Generously cover the fish with the hot pastis stock, arrange the vegetables over the fish and sprinkle with the thyme powder and chopped fennel greenery.

spaghetti with a swordfish-vegetable-ragout

1 COURGETTE (ZUCCHINI)
1/2 AUBERGINE
2 TOMATOES, SKINNED AND PIPS REMOVED
2 ARTICHOKE BASES SNIP OFF THE TIPS & FINELY CUT UP THE LEAVES
100 G CAULIFLOWER & SALT
1/2 SHALLOT, CHOPPED
1 GARLIC CLOVE WITH SKIN
100 G OLIVE OIL
150 G SWORD FISH, SKINNED AND BONED
20 G CAPERS
240 G SPAGHETTI
1 BUNCH BASIL
PEPERONCINO (SMALL, RED CHILLI PEPPER)

Finely cube the courgette, aubergine and tomatoes. Steam the artichoke pieces, divide the cauliflower into florets and boil in salted water.

Sauté the shallots and the garlic in oil. Add the aubergine and stir-fry, then add all the other vegetables.

Cut the sword fish into small pieces, fry lightly and add to the vegetables. Season the ragout with capers.

Cook the spaghetti and add it to the fish-and-vegetable-ragout. Fold in the chopped basil leaves and flavour with peperoncino before serving on hot plates.

orecchiette with anchovies

360 G ORECCHIETTE
(SMALL, SHELL SHAPED PASTA)
200 G TOMATO CUBES
200 G BROCCOLI
2–3 T OLIVE OIL
1–2 GARLIC CLOVES, PRESSED
1 ANCHOVY FILET, CHOPPED
BASIL LEAVES
SALT & FRESHLY GROUND PEPPER
50 G PARMESAN CHEESE

Boil the orecchiette in salted water. After 5 minutes, add the cleaned broccoli and boil together for apx. 15 minutes. Pour off the water and allow draining – reserve some of the liquid for the sauce.

Heat the olive oil and add the garlic, tomato pieces and chopped basil. Season with salt, pepper and the chopped anchovy filet. Simmer for 5 minutes then fill in some of the pasta liquid, thereafter the orecchiette and the broccoli. Sauté in pan and season to taste.

Spread grease-proof paper on a plate, centre the orecchiette and seal the paper by folding it (twice around the edges). Bake in a hot oven for 2 – 3 minutes.

When serving the orecchiette is brought to the table inside its paper. This parcel is then opened and the pasta is served onto plates and the freshly grated parmesan is offered.

Grilled tuna on lentils with tomato vinaigrette

For the lentils
2 T olive oil
2 T onion, finely chopped
2 T carrot, finely chopped
2 T white celery, finely chopped
250 g green lentils, sorted,
rinsed and soaked overnight

For the vinaigrette
1 T red wine vinegar
1/2 tsp dried red chilli pepper, pounded
100 ml native olive oil
sea salt & freshly ground pepper
2 ripe tomatoes, skinned,
pips removed and finely cubed

2 T olive oil
4 tuna fish steaks (each about 200 g)
sea salt & freshly ground pepper

Fry the onion, carrot and celery in 2 T of olive oil for apx. 5 minutes at a medium setting. Add the lentils and cover with water (7.5 cm deep) and bring to boil. Allow to simmer without the lid for about 25 minutes. Pour off the water and keep warm. Pre-heat the electric grill.

Mix the ingredients for vinaigrette together in a bowl.

Brush the grill grid with oil, lay the tuna steaks onto the grill and brush the remaining oil. Grill each side for 2-4 minutes and season with salt and freshly ground pepper.

Dish the lentils onto 4 pre-warmed plates and place the tuna steaks on top. Pour over some vinaigrette and serve.

Tuna steaks in almond relish

4 tuna steaks, 200 g each
salt, pepper (shredded pink pepper if desired)
1 garlic, halved
1 lemon, sliced
2 bay leaves
1 sprig rosemary
1 T salted butter
olive oil

For the relish
40 g sliced almonds
2 spring onions
1 garlic clove
1 chilli pod
40 g raisins
lemon juice
olive oil
salt, pepper
2 sprigs basil
1 onion

Warm up the olive oil. Season the tuna steaks with salt and pepper and place them in the pan. Add the garlic, lemon slices, rosemary and bay leaves and fry. Just before the ingredients are cooked, add the butter.

For the relish: Cut the spring onions, garlic, onion and the chilli pods into small pieces and briefly fry them in olive oil. Add the raisins and the almonds.

Season with salt, pepper and lemon juice. Finally sprinkle in the chopped basil.

Serve the tuna with the relish.

Risotto with lampuki tatare

300 g risotto rice
2 T olive oil
1 T butter
1 dl dry white wine
100 g onions, chopped
4 garlic cloves, finely chopped
1 T tomato paste
1 T ketchup
salt
pepper
1 l vegetable or poultry broth
1 red pepper, cut into small pieces
100 g hard goats' cheese, grated

Lightly fry the olive oil, butter, garlic, onions and red pepper, tomato paste and ketchup. Add the rice and pour in the white wine. Gradually add the warm broth and simmer until the rice is cooked (about 25 minutes). Season to taste and fold in the goats' cheese. Using an ice-cream scoop, form round balls.

Lampuki tatare

300 g lampuki fillet, skinned & boned.
Remove the sinews and cut into pieces.
juice of 1 lime or lemon
salt
white pepper
1 pepperoni, remove the pips
cut into small pieces
ca. 50 g rocket lettuce,
rinsed and cut into small pieces
1 onion, cut into small pieces
4 rosemary sprigs, finely chopped
1/2 tsp honey

Mix the above ingredients together and serve the lampuki tatare with the risotto balls

Tomato-basil sherbet on a cucumber jelly with langostino cakes

For 4–6 servings

1 kg cucumbers
salt, pepper & Cayenne
juice of half a lemon
2 sheets gelatine
Vietnamese coriander, finely chopped

For the tomato sherbet

10-12 medium-sized ripe tomatoes
salt & white pepper
basil
garlic, unpeeled
olive oil
basil leaves to puree
90 g glucose

For the langostino cakes

500 g fillet of sole
250 g cream, ice-cold
salt, pepper & Pernod
15 small langostinos (prawns), shelled and cut into pieces
50 g white bread croutons, fried golden brown
100 g boiled vegetable pieces (e.g. carrots, celery, and courgettes)
Vietnamese coriander

Peel the cucumbers and season with salt, pepper and Cayenne. Add the lemon juice and finely chopped coriander and puree in mixer for 2-3 minutes. Hang a cheese cloth over a bowl and strain the puree through this, leave to drain in the fridge. Mix the dissolved gelatine with half a litre of cucumber juice and return to the fridge to cool.

Preparing the tomato sherbet: Blanch the tomatoes, peel, cut into quarters and remove the pips. Lay the tomatoes out on a baking tray and seasoning with basil, salt, pepper, olive oil and garlic which has been crushed inside its skin. Dry in the oven at 60 °C for 4-5 hours. Puree the dried tomatoes (about 600 g) with the basil. Fold in the glucose and freeze in an ice-cream machine.

Preparing the fish cakes: Puree the cooled fish fillets and ice-cold cream very finely in a blender. Place the mixture on ice and season with salt, pepper and a dash of Pernod. Add the prawns, croutons and the vegetable pieces and carefully (this spice is very intensive) flavour with the finely chopped coriander. Form the fish cakes.
Heat a little oil in a pan and fry the fish cakes on both sides until they are golden-brown, finish cooking the cakes by placing them under the grill for 2-3 minutes.

To serve, arrange the tomato-basil sherbet on the cucumber jelly and serve together with the fish cakes.

Sole with spinach

2 fresh Soles (Seezungen) (500 g each)
750 g fresh spinach
1/2 lemon (juice)
2 garlic cloves
2 T dry white wine
2 T butter
freshly grated Parmesan cheese (optional)
salt & freshly ground pepper

For the sauce
1 small onion
1 tsp fresh thyme leaves (or 1/2 tsp dried thyme leaves)
2 T butter
250 ml milk
200 g cream
2 egg yolks
3 T freshly grated Parmesan cheese
1 1/2 T flour
salt, freshly ground pepper

Fillet the soles (your fishmonger may prepare them for you) by placing the fish with the dark side up on your working surface. Remove the side fins with a kitchen scissors. To skin the fish cut a slit the across the tail. In one clean stroke pull the skin from the tail to the head. Turn the fish over and remove the paler skin in the same way. Using a sharp knife with a thin, flexible blade slit along both sides of the backbone. Then cut the fillet away from the bones and the head and gently lift of the fillets. Lightly season the 8 fillets with salt and pepper, and then trickle the lemon over the top.

Wash the spinach leaves and allow them to drip dry. Heat the spinach in a saucepan with the white wine, salt and pepper. Add the juice of 2 garlic cloves, put the lid on the saucepan and cook until the spinach leaves fall together.

For the sauce: Finely chop up the little onion and glaze in a tablespoon of butter. Sprinkle in a teaspoon of thyme leaves; pour in 250 ml of milk and season with salt and pepper. Briefly bring to boil and then leave to draw for about 5 minutes.

Gently melt a tablespoon of butter in a saucepan, add the flour and blend into the butter to make a smooth roux. Gradually add the cream and the thyme-flavoured milk and simmer, stirring continuously, until creamy. Remove the sauce from heat and stir in the egg yolks and the Parmesan cheese. Season with salt and pepper.

Polipo mosaic with olive sauce

1 polipo (octopus), medium size
bay leaves
5 l fish stock
4 T pesto
4 T Taggia olives, stoned
Extra vergine olive oil
Salt & pepper
pine nuts, roasted

For the seafood stock
6 l water
2 carrots
2 celery stalks
1 onion
1-2 l white wine vinegar
10 bay leaves
1 handful rough sea salt

For the pesto
100 g basil
100 g extra vergine olive oil
10 g pine nuts
10 g walnuts
10 g Parmesan cheese

Preparing the pesto: Puree the basil with oil, pine nuts, walnuts and parmesan in the mixer, push through a fine sieve and leave to cool in the fridge until just before serving.

Clean and halve the polipo lengthwise down the middle and then put it back together again. »Spike« bay leaves into octopus and make a small »meatloaf« and fasten it with kitchen thread.

Preparing the stock: Add the vinegar, salt, vegetables and bay leaves to the water and boil for about an hour till the liquid has been reduced to apx. 5 l. Add the octopus and boil for another 2 hours, then leave to cool in the stock. Remove the polipo and wrap it so tightly in transparent foil that a cylindrical shape is formed. Cool in the fridge overnight.

Preparing the sauce: Puree the olives with the olive oil.

To serve, cut the cooled octopus into slices and serve it with olive sauce, pesto and roasted pine nuts.

Red mullet fillets with tomato-risotto

4 red mullet fillets
salt, pepper, lemon
oil for frying
rocket lettuce for garnishing

For the sauce

100 g butter
salt & cayenne pepper
200 g rocket lettuce
oil for frying
100 g sliced onions
20 g butter
200 g potatoes,
peeled and cut into thin slices
1 garlic clove, pressed
lemon
750 ml chicken stock

For the risotto

30 g chopped shallots
butter & white wine
150 g risotto rice
400 g tomato consommé
salt, pepper & lemon
80 g oven-baked tomato quarters

Preparing the sauce: Whisk the butter till creamy and season with salt and cayenne pepper. Wash the salad, allow to dry and very briefly deep-fry in hot oil (at 180 °C) for about 30 seconds. The leaves should be crisp but stay green, lay these on a cloth and squeeze out the excess fat. Chop the leaves into powder and fold this into the creamy butter.

Lightly fry the onion slices in butter, add the potatoes and garlic and briefly sauté. Season with salt, cayenne pepper and lemon. Top up with chicken stock and simmer at a low setting until the potatoes are soft. Press the potato stock through a fine sieve, season to taste and turn in the rocket butter (apx. 50 g butter to 200 g potato stock).

Preparing the risotto: Lightly fry the shallots in butter, then add a dash of white wine and stir-fry the rice until it becomes glazy. Gradually fill in the tomato consommé, add the rice and cook for 18–20 minutes, stirring constantly. Season the risotto with salt, pepper and lemon and fold in the oven-baked tomatoes.

Season fish fillets with salt, pepper and lemon. Heat a little oil in a coated frying pan, and place fillets (with skin side down) in the hot oil. Place the pan under a hot grill for 2 minutes, thus the fish will remain juicy, and the skin intact and the red colour is maintained.

Arrange the red mullet fillets on the tomato-risotto pour the sauce around and garnish with rocket leaves.

Prawns with melon, Chinese chives and honey

2 l salt-free chicken broth
20 fresh prawns
4 T soy sauce
150 ml Shaoxing rice wine
(as an alternative use fino sherry)
40 stalks Chinese garlic chives
8-12 T melon balls (equal amounts
of honeydew, Crenshaw and watermelon)
4 Chilli peppers,
without pips and finely cut up
2 T peanut oil
1 T woodland honey
(with an intensive flavour)
1/2 lemon
salt
2 T corn-flour,
stirred into a little water

Boil up the chicken broth and continue boiling until the amount of liquid has been reduced to about a 250 ml. Season with salt, if necessary.

Shell the prawns, remove the digestive tracts and break off tails if desired. Marinate the prawns in 4 tablespoons of shoaxing wine and soy sauce for 4-5 minutes. Finely chop up the Chinese chives. Prepare the melon balls, chilli pieces and plates since the cooking time is short and the dish must be served quickly so that the crisp freshness is not lost.

Strongly heat-up the wok or cast-iron pan, take the prawns out of the marinade and, together with the peanut oil, put them in the smouldering hot wok. Briefly stir-fry until the prawns curl up and brownish fry-marks are visible.

Add the melon balls, the remaining wine and the reduced chicken broth to the pan. Stir in the honey, fold in the garlic and chilli and boil up once more. Thicken with the dissolved corn flour and flavour with lemon juice and salt. Serve on the plates.

Rocket gazpacho with salmon sherbet und scampi

100 g rocket
100 g spinach leaves, blanched
100 g green courgette skins
100 g olive oil
1 T finely ground hazel nuts
salt, pepper
lemon juice

4 scampi, skinned
salt, pepper
olive oil, butter

For the sherbet
200 g graved salmon
20 ml vodka
200 g cream
30 g milk
3 egg yolks
3 egg whites
lemon, salt & pepper
Worcestershire sauce

Puree the rocket, spinach leaves and courgette skins in a mixer and whip up with the olive oil, stir in the hazel nuts, seasoning with salt, pepper and lemon juice and leave to cool.

Cut the salmon into chunks and puree it with the vodka in a kitchen blender. Add milk and cream to the salmon puree and bring to boil, allow to draw for 10 minutes before pushing the puree through a sieve and flavouring with salt, pepper and lemon juice.

Place the bowl over hot water (bain-marie) and beat the egg yolk till it is foamy. Remove from heat and add the salmon puree and beat them together until stiff. Season once more. Beat egg whites till they are semi-stiff and gently fold under the salmon before freezing.

Season the scampi and fry them in a mix of olive oil and butter. Spread the rocket leaves onto cooled plates and lightly dress with salt and olive oil. Fill in the gazpacho and arrange the salmon sherbet and scampi on the side.

Cavatelli pasta with clams

320 G CAVATELLI PASTA, BLACK & WHITE
400 G CLAMS
1 GARLIC CLOVE
1 SHALLOT, CHOPPED UP
2 T OLIVE OIL
50 ML WHITE WINE
40 G CALAMARETTI (SMALL SQUIDS)
OLIVE OIL
1 GARLIC CLOVE, CHOPPED
40 G TOMATO CONCASSÉ
(ROUGHLY CHOPPED TOMATOES)
1 T SMOOTH PARSLEY, CHOPPED
PEPERONCINO OIL
BASIL LEAVES FOR GARNISHING

For the cavatelli pasta

300 G POTATOES
1 KG FLOUR
1 EGG
30 ML LUKEWARM WATER
SALT, PEPPER
10 SMALL SQUID INK BAGS

Preparing the cavatelli: Boil the potatoes till they are soft, remove the skins and push the potatoes through a sieve. Add the flour, egg and water to the potatoes and knead together, seasoning with salt and pepper. Dye half of the pasta dough with the squid ink. Separately knead both halves of the dough (as for a pizza), wrap them in transparent foil and stand for 2 hours.

Using a pasta rolling pin, roll out the dough till it is 1 cm thick, cut into 1 cm wide strips and roll these into sausage shapes – always flouring well. Cut these rolls into pieces of 5 cm; press them down lightly with your thumb. Place the cavatelli in the fridge until needed (uncooked cavatelli can be stored in the freezer)

Boil the black and white cavatelli in salted water for 8-10 minutes and then drain.

Clean the mussels and lightly brown them with the garlic, shallots and olive oil. Pour in the white wine and leave to draw on the stove for 2-3 minutes with the lid on. Take out the mussels and open the shell to remove the insides. Pour the stock through a sieve and keep it for later.

Wash the calamaretti and cut into thin rings. Heat the olive oil in a saucepan; add the chopped garlic and the calamaretti fill in the mussel stock.

Fold in the mussels, tomato-concassé, chopped parsley and the drained cavatelli. Pep up with a few drops of sharp peperoncino oil.

Serve in soup dishes garnished with basil.

Chicken legs marinated in lemon and mustard

2 GARLIC CLOVES
5 T CHOPPED; MIXED HERBS (E.G. ROSEMARY, BASIL, PARSLEY AND THYME)
100 ML LEMON JUICE
ZEST OF LEMON (CHEMICALLY UNTREATED)
2 T OLIVE OIL
2 T LIQUID HONEY
5 T HOT MUSTARD
SALT
BLACK PEPPER
8 CHICKEN LEGS

Peel and press the garlic and mix it with the herbs, lemon juice, lemon zest, oil, liquid honey, hot mustard, salt and plenty of black pepper.

Rinse and dry the chicken legs. Place the chicken into the marinade, turning to coat well. Cover and leave to draw in the fridge for about 2 hours, turn occasionally.

Pre-heat a barbecue or an electric grill. Remove chicken legs from marinade and dab them dry. Barbecue or grill each side for about 8-10 minutes, repeatedly brushing on more marinade.

Chicken in garlic sauce

900 G CHICKEN BREAST FILETS
FLOUR, SEASONED WITH SALT AND PEPPER
4 T OLIVE OIL
4 T BUTTER
5-6 T WHITE WINE
4 T CHICKEN STOCK
3 TSP CHOPPED GARLIC
1 T CHOPPED PARSLEY
1 LARGE T SHERRY
1 LARGE T BRANDY
SALT AND FRESHLY GROUND PEPPER
PARSLEY FOR GARNISHING

Cut up the chicken into small pieces and coat with the seasoned flour.

Heat the oil and the butter in a saucepan and fry the chicken fillets, turning frequently, until they are evenly golden brown all over.

Add the wine, chicken stock, chopped garlic and parsley and simmer until the liquid has been reduced to about half its former volume. Stir in the sherry and brandy.

Season to taste with salt and pepper and garnish with parsley leaves before serving.

Cold pork medallions in saffron jelly

600 g pork filet,
remove the skin and sinews,
cut into pieces (medallions)
of about 80-100 g
6 sage leaves
6 bay leaves
4 garlic cloves
4 T olive oil
2 T butter

salt
white pepper, freshly ground
5 g saffron threads
200 g dry white wine
1 T prickly pear liqueur
2 sheets gelatine, soaked in water and dissolved
1 mild, red pepperoni without the pips, cut into small pieces

Heat the olive oil and the butter in a saucepan and fry pork medallions on both sides for about 3 minutes until pink. Add the sage, bay leaves and garlic, and flavour with salt and pepper. Add the saffron, prickly pear liqueur and white wine and braise for 2 minutes. Remove the medallions and put them in the fridge.

Strain the stock through a sieve; fold in the gelatine and pepperoni bits. Cool the gelatine in the fridge before pouring it over the medallions.

Veal roulades with an artichoke filling

4 x 200 g veal roulades
(lengths thinly cut from the inner leg)
mustard as desired
4 slices smoked bacon
4 white bread croutons, fried in butter
and apx. 5 cm long each
salt, freshly ground white pepper
2 T olive oil

For the marinade

700 ml red wine
120 g chopped onions
80 g celery stalks, cut into pieces
80 g carrots, cut into pieces
15 crushed peppercorns
1 each bay leaf and thyme sprig
2 cloves
1 T sugar

For the artichoke filling

60 g shallots
60 g Parma ham
8 fresh artichoke hearts
100 g mushrooms
10 g butter
pressed garlic clove
1 tsp mild mustard
20 ml Noilly Prat (dry white vermouth)
100 ml cream
4 basil leaves
1 T finely chopped parsley

For the Sauce

20 g butter
1 T tomato paste
30 g cold knobs of butter

Cut the roulades. Place the ingredients into a dish and immerse the meat. Leave to marinate overnight. On the following day, remove the slices of meat from the marinade and dab them dry. Strain the red wine marinade through a sieve and boil up the liquid. Skim off the foam. Set aside the vegetables and the contents of the sieve.

For the stuffing: Finely chop up the shallots and ham, cut the artichoke hearts and mushrooms into larger pieces. Lightly brown the shallots in the butter and continue to fry, adding first the ham and then the artichokes and mushrooms. Stir in the garlic, mustard, vermouth and cream and boil down the liquid. Season with finely chopped herbs, salt and pepper. Spread this stuffing onto the meat slices and roll them up, hold them together with kitchen thread, making sure the ends are well closed so that the stuffing can't fall out during cooking.

Season meat rolls with salt and pepper and brown them on all sides in a metal roasting pan with 2 T of oil. Add the herbs and vegetables from the marinade and fry these too. Fill in red wine marinade, close the lid and braise for 1 hour in the pre-heated oven at 180 °C. The heat should come from the top and the bottom. If there is not enough red wine, add with some water. After removing the herbs, press the sauce and the vegetables through a sieve. Boil down the liquid till the desired consistency is reached, then stir in the cold pats of butter and season with salt and pepper.

Beef stew with chocolate vegetables

- 2 red pepper (about 300 g)
- 1 large fleshy tomato (about 250 g)
- 2 garlic cloves
- 1 onion
- 50 g bittersweet dark chocolate
- 3 T vinegar
- 3 T oil
- 800 g stewing beef, cut into chunks
- salt
- black pepper, freshly ground
- 375 ml meat stock
- 2 cloves
- 1/2 cinnamon stick
- 2 large carrots (about 250 g)
- 1 large potato (about 200 g)

Pre-heat the oven to 250 °C. Bake the peppers on the middle shelf for apx. 20 minutes until cooked. Halve the peppers and remove the skin and the pips, then cut up the flesh.

While the peppers are baking, skin the tomatoes by pouring boiling water over; also remove the pips and the stem before cutting up the flesh. Peel the garlic and the onion and cut the onion into quarters. Break the chocolate into pieces. Puree the paprika, tomatoes, garlic, chocolate and vinegar in the mixer.

Heat the oil and brown meat (portion by portion) and season with salt and pepper. Add the puree, stock, cloves and cinnamon, and then simmer with the lid on for apx. 50 minutes till the meat is tender.

Peel and rinse the carrots and potatoes. Cut the carrots into quarters lengthwise and then cut into small pieces, also cut the potatoes into cubes. Add the carrots and potatoes to the meat and continue to simmer for another 15 minutes. Remove the cloves and the cinnamon and then season the stew.

summer vegetable couscous

Seasonal summer vegetables,
300 g per person e.g. navets (turnips),
mini-carrots, mini-fennel,
yellow and green mini courgettes
100 g couscous (tiny grains of
semolina flour, served like rice),
not parboiled

For the sauce
40 ml extra vergine olive oil
1 garlic clove
1 tin tomato pieces
2 large tomatoes, peeled, pips removed
and cut into pieces
mint leaves, plucked off the stem
ginger root, peeled and finely cut up
bay leaf, crushed
curry powder, cinnamon powder
nutmeg, grated
coriander, ground
black pepper, ground

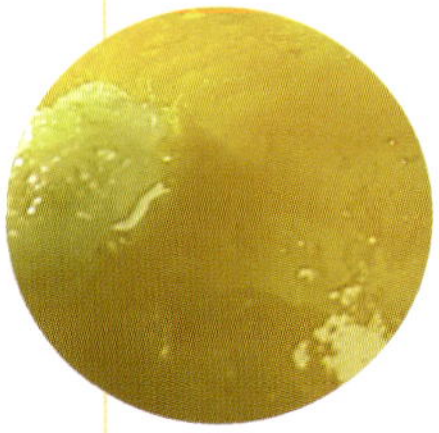

Cut all the vegetables into small cubes, rings or strips; you need at least 2 tablespoons of each vegetable type. In a suitable saucepan, boil up a minimum of 1 l of slightly salted water. Using a sieve, separately blanch the different sorts of mini vegetables in this boiling water, then remove them and immerse in cold water. The water used to boil the vegetables should be kept for later.

Preparing the sauce: Heat the olive oil in a pan, add the garlic and the tomatoes (both tinned and fresh) and fry lightly. Add the finely cut up herbs, some ginger and the bay leaf, season with a large pinch of each of the powdered spices. Simmer for about 20 minutes. Before serving, thin down the puree-like consistency with apx. 4 tablespoons of vegetable water.

Rinse the couscous twice and allow draining. Boil in a couscous pot in the classic way.

Spread the tomato sauce on the serving plates, arrange the couscous in a circle on the sauce and decorate by scattering the vegetables over.

Courgette and herb flan

1 onion
1-2 garlic cloves
2-3 sage leaves
1 sprig rosmary
1 courgette (300– 400 g)
2 T olive oil
200 g cream
4 eggs
50 g Parmesan, freshly grated
salt
1 pinch nutmeg
oil to grease the form

Peel both the onion and the garlic clove and cut them into small pieces. Rinse the sage and rosemary, pluck the needles and leaves from the stems and chop up finely. Wash the courgette and cut it into thin slices.

Heat the oil in a pot and briefly stir-fry the onion and the garlic till they are golden-yellow. Add the sage, rosemary and courgette and smoulder for 1 – 2 minutes. Pour in the cream and allow cooking at medium heat. Remove from the stove and leave to cool off a little.

Pre-heat the oven to 180 °C. Fill a large pan or another heat-proof container with water and place it in the oven. Grease the casserole with oil.

Separate the eggs. Stir the egg yolk into the Parmesan and the courgette blend and season with salt, pepper and nutmeg.

Beat the egg white till it is stiff and gently fold under the courgette blend. Fill the mixture into the greased form and place this form into the bed of hot water inside the oven (convectional 160 °C) for 30-35 minutes till the flan has solidified and is golden-brown on top.

Artichoke and watercress terrine with tomato vinaigrette

For 4–6 portions

8 ARTICHOKES
SALT AND FRESHLY GROUND PEPPER
LEMON JUICE
WHITE WINE VINEGAR, LEMON & OIL
2 BUNCHES WATERCRESS
3 SHEETS GELATINE

FOR THE VINAIGRETTE
1–2 FLESHY TOMATOES, SKINNED, PIPS REMOVED AND CUT INTO PIECES
WHITE WINE VINEGAR, LEMON AND OIL
1 SHALLOT, CHOPPED
SALT AND PEPPER
SUGAR

Separate the artichoke hearts from the stem and the choke. Boil the hearts in salted water with some lemon juice until they are tender, remove from the water and allow cooling. Mix the vinegar, oil, salt, pepper and lemon into a marinade and leave artichoke hearts to marinate for 2 hours.

Clean and rinse the watercress, then blanch, immerse in iced water and allow draining. Using the kitchen mixer, blend the cress and 3–4 artichoke hearts into a fine puree. Season with salt, pepper and lemon and then stir in the dissolved gelatine.

Fill the puree into a dish and layer with the rest of the artichoke hearts, cool for 4–6 hours. Turn out artichoke and watercress terrine onto a platter and cut into slices.

Prepare tomato vinaigrette from ingredients listed above and serve this with the watercress terrine.

Filled tomatoes

6 round tomatoes with stalks
(diameter about 6 cm)
2 small, white spring onions,
finely chopped
1 T mixed herbs
(basil, parsley, coriander)
olive oil
sherry vinegar
salt, pepper

Peel the tomatoes without removing stalks (for garnishing later). Cut off the lids of 4 of the tomatoes and scoop out the seeds and flesh. Sprinkle salt on the tomatoes (both inside and out) so that they exude some fluid. Cut the flesh of the 2 remaining tomatoes into small pieces, lightly salt and allow draining. Mix in the chopped spring onions and herbs, then season to taste with olive oil, sherry vinegar, salt and pepper. Dry the hollowed-out tomatoes by dabbing with a paper towel and fill them with the tomato-herb mixture. Arrange the tomatoes on a plate and serve.

Pickled cherry tomatoes

1 kg cherry tomatoes,
without stalk, with slit skins
1 l water
125 ml white wine vinegar
3 bay leaves
1 dill sprig
some parsley sprigs
some black peppercorns
salt
2 cinnamon sticks
4 garlic cloves
3 T brown sugar
1 T honey
1 T mustard seeds

Mix all ingredients (except the cherry tomatoes) together, briefly heat them up and then leave to cool.

Add the cherry tomatoes, and leave to stand for 3-4 days (covered) in a cold place.

Tomato chutney

750 g tomatoes
250 g onions
2 fresh chilli peppers
3 T oil
6 cloves
150 ml red wine vinegar
150 g brown sugar
salt
white pepper, freshly ground
nutmeg, freshly grated

Slit the tomato skins and scald them with boiling water, then immerse them in cold water and remove the skins. Cut tomatoes into quarters, remove the pips and cut the flesh into small cubes. Peel the onions and dice them. Cut the chilli peppers lengthwise, remove the pips and cut into little pieces.

Heat the oil in a large saucepan and glaze the onions in it. Add the tomatoes, chillies, cloves, vinegar, sugar and spices and boil at medium heat for apx. 20 minutes, stirring occasionally. Leave the tomato chutney to cool down.

This tomato chutney goes well with grilled pork, veal or turkey meat.

Tomato compote

4 tomatoes,
skinned and pips removed
50-60 g dried tomatoes
1 T onions, chopped
1 garlic clove
40 g butter
1 sprig of thyme
1 bay leaf
orange powder (made of dried orange peel, cut up in a mixer)
sugar, salt & Parmesan cheese
black pepper

Cut up both the fresh and the dried tomatoes into cubes. Glaze the onions and garlic in the butter. Add the tomato pieces, thyme and bay leaf to fry at a low setting until the liquid has evaporated and a fairly solid, mouldable, mixture has been created.

Season the compote with a pinch of orange powder, sugar, salt and pepper. Serve in a pyramid shape and garnish with Parmesan cheese slices which have been cut into thin triangles.

Tomato-orange sauce with spaghetti

1 kg ripe tomatoes
2 T olive oil
2 garlic cloves
2 T fresh plain-leaved parsley, finely chopped
2 T fresh Thai basil leaves, finely chopped
1 tsp fresh oregano
sea salt
freshly ground white pepper
2 oranges
700 g spaghetti
60 g freshly grated Parmesan cheese

To skin the tomatoes, remove the stems and slit a small cross into the skins, place the tomatoes onto a skimmer and briefly hold into boiling water. Skin and peel the tomatoes, also remove the pips and cut the tomatoes into small pieces. Work over a fine sieve and a porcelain bowl so that the lost juice can be caught up.

Heat the olive oil in a tall, stainless-steel frying-pan and briefly fry the garlic cloves, parsley and basil. Add the tomato juice, tomato pieces and the oregano and stir in with a wooden cooking spoon. Simmer at a very low setting for 20 minutes, continue to stir constantly to dissolve the tomatoes. Flavour with salt and pepper.

Squeeze out the oranges and press the juice via a fine sieve, into the sauce. Boil the sauce for another 5 minutes at a medium heat. Press the sauce through a fine sieve into a sauteuse (deep frying-pan) and whisk strongly. Allow it to simmer for 2 minutes.

Fill the sauce into a white porcelain bowl and add the freshly cooked spaghetti. Mix them together and sprinkle Parmesan over the top, serve immediately while still hot.

Lemon and garlic potatoes

800 g small potatoes
salt
2 lemons
1 T vinegar
2 T meat broth
1 bunch parsley
black pepper, freshly ground
8 garlic cloves
6 T cold-pressed olive oi

Clean the potatoes with a brush under running water. Boil in the potatoes (unpeeled) in a covered pot of salt water for apx. 25 minutes (or until cooked).

Pour off the water, and peel the potatoes when they have cooled a bit. Cut into slices of 2 cm while the potatoes are still lukewarm.

Press the lemons and pour the juice into a bowl. Mix the lemon juice with vinegar and meat broth. Wash the parsley and shake off the excess water, chop up the leaves and fold it in, seasoning with salt and pepper.

Peel and chop up the garlic and add it, together with the olive oil, to the lemon sauce. Whisk the ingredients together.

Pour the sauce over the lukewarm potatoes and serve.

Sardine paste

6 boned sardines (tinned)
1 onion
1/2 bunch plain parsley
4 T mayonnaise
1 tsp lime juice
salt & freshly ground pepper
green olives
oven-fresh Maltese white bread

Remove the sardines from the tin and briefly rinse under cold water. Dab dry with kitchen paper and chop up finely.

Skin the onion and chop into fine cubes. Wash the parsley and pluck the leaves from the stem then chop up finely.

Mix the sardines, onion, parsley and mayonnaise together, then season with lime juice, salt and freshly ground pepper. Serve sardine paste with olives and fresh white bread.

sweet and sour aubergines

ingredients for 4 – 6 servings

600 G AUBERGINES
3 STALKS CELERY
200 G MILD WHITE ONIONS
1 BUNCH BASIL
1 LARGE TIN PEELED TOMATOES
50 G GREEN OLIVES, STONED
2 T CAPERS
5 – 6 T WHITE WINE VINEGAR
CA. 100 ML OLIVE OIL
1/2 TSP SUGAR
SALT & FRESHLY GROUND PEPPER

Cut the aubergines into cubes of apx. 1 cm and place them in a sieve. Sprinkle with salt and set aside for about 1 hour to draw out the bitterness.

Clean the celery stalks and cut into pieces of 3 cm. Lay aside the tender green leaves for garnishing later. Chop the onions into large pieces. Drain the tinned tomatoes and cut them into small pieces (the juice is not needed for this recipe and can be used for another dish e.g. for making a soup). Cut the olives in half.

Heat 4 tablespoons of olive oil in a wide saucepan and glaze the onions. Add the celery pieces and fry for a few minutes. Sprinkle with 1/2 tsp of sugar and flavour with salt and pepper. Stir in the tomatoes, olives and capers and cook in an open saucepan for 15 minutes at the lowest setting, stirring occasionally.

Meanwhile, rinse the aubergines briefly and dab dry with kitchen paper. Heat the rest of the olive oil to a high temperature in a pan. Fry portions of the aubergines until they are crisp and drain on the kitchen paper, repeat this procedure till the all of the aubergines are crisp.

Add the aubergine fritters to the vegetables in the saucepan and add 5 tablespoons of white wine vinegar. Allow to simmer for 15 minutes more and then season with salt, pepper and perhaps a little more vinegar.

Before serving, garnish with fresh basil leaves and chopped celery leaves.

DESSERTS

sweet dishes

Desserts

Pastries, cakes & biscuits

Chocolate noodles and sour cherries

Ingredients for pasta
250 g wheat flour
100 g cacao powder
30 g icing sugar
1 vanilla pod
4 eggs

Sour cherries
350 g sour cherries (in a glass)
10 g corn-flour
40 g sugar
1 cinnamon stick
1 clove

Vanilla cream
125 ml cream
20 g icing sugar
1 vanilla pod with contents scratched out

Garnishing
mint leaves

Sift the flour and the cacao powder onto the working surface. Make a hollow in the centre and put the icing sugar and contents of vanilla pod inside. Beat the eggs and fill them into the hollow, then knead the ingredients into smooth dough. Wrap foil around the dough and allow resting for about 30 minutes. Roll out the dough until it is 3 mm thick. The rolling could also be done by a pasta-making machine; here the dough would be rolled out several times until the required thinness is reached. This is done by adjusting the rollers (closer each time), set the ribbon width at apx. 3 mm for the final cutting.

Place the noodles on a cloth and allow them to dry briefly.

Place a sieve over a bowl and measure off 125 ml of the juice and put some cherries aside for garnishing later. Stir the corn-flour into 2 tablespoons of juice till it dissolves. Boil up the rest of the juice in a saucepan with the sugar, cinnamon and the clove. Stir in the corn-flour and continuously stir with a whisk continuously as the liquid thickens. When the juice is bound, stir in the cherries and remove the cinnamon and the clove, put them aside for later.

For the vanilla cream: Beat the cream, icing sugar and contents of the vanilla pod together.

Boil the pasta in slightly salted, bubbling water till it is »al dente«. Lift the pasta out with a skimmer and serve into soup dishes, cover with vanilla cream and garnish with some cherries and mint leaves.

As a variation to the vanilla cream you could use a vanilla sauce.

Tip *the cacao dough becomes very sticky, so scatter plenty of flour over it when rolling (applies to both rolling pin and machine). Naturally it is advisable to let the dough dry well before cooking it.*

stacked pancakes with a caramelized crust

For 6 to 8 persons

For the pancakes

175 g flour
320 ml milk
2 eggs
zest of 1/2 lemon
seeds of 1 vanilla pod
salt
100 g butter concentrate for frying

For the filling

80 g butter
110 g sugar
250 g curd cheese
3 egg yolks
1 T crème fraîche (sour cream)
zest of 1/2 orange and 1/2 lemon
50 g raisins
salt
1 T honey liqueur
2 egg whites

For the topping

40 g sugar
1 egg
1 egg white
125 g whipping cream
seeds of 1 vanilla pod
2 T brown sugar

For the batter: Mix the flour, milk, eggs, lemon zest, vanilla and a pinch of salt in a bowl.

Brush the butter concentrate into a hot frying pan (Ø 26 cm). Ladle some batter into the pan and carefully tilt the pan so that the batter is evenly spread. When the pancake is golden brown underneath, turn it over and fry the other side. Make 6 pancakes in this way, brushing butter around the pan before each one. Put the finished pancakes aside.

For the filling: Beat 60 g butter and 50 g sugar together until foamy. Gradually fold in the curd cheese, egg yolk and crème fraîche. Add orange and lemon zest and season with a pinch of salt and honey liqueur. Fold in the raisins. Beat the egg whites and the rest of the sugar until stiff and then fold in.

Brush out a cake tin (Ø 26 cm) with a thick layer of the remaining butter. Place a pancake into it and spread on some filling, then place another pancake on top and spread on some more filling, continuing in this way until the pancakes and the filling have been used up. A plain pancake without filling must be on top.

Bake the pancake-layers in a pre-heated oven at 200 °C for 10-12 minutes.

Meanwhile, prepare the topping by stirring sugar, egg and egg white together, pour in the cream and fold in the vanilla.

Evenly spread the egg topping over the cake and bake for a further 20 minutes at the same temperature.

Scatter the brown sugar over the topping and allow it to caramelize for about 5-6 minutes. Remove the »cake« from the oven and allow cooling. When it is tepid, take the cake from the baking tin and cut into slices.

Potato-pancake with aniseed-apple sauce

Ingredients for 2 persons

FOR THE POTATO PANCAKE PIECES
- 500 G FLOURY POTATOES, BOILED
- 75 G SEMOLINA
- SALT
- 100 G CURD CHEESE OR COTTAGE CHEESE
- 1 EGG
- 2-3 T BUTTER CONCENTRATE

FOR THE ANISEED AND APPLE SAUCE
- 600 G SOUR COOKING APPLES
- 1 T LEMON JUICE
- 1-2 T SUGAR
- 1 PINCH CINNAMON POWDER
- 1 TSP ANISEED LIQUEUR

For the aniseed-apple sauce: Peel, quarter and de-core the apples and cut into chunky pieces. Mix the apples with lemon juice, sugar and cinnamon in a saucepan and bring to the boil. Cover and simmer for about 25 minutes until the apples are well cooked and soft. Stir the apples firmly and press them into a puree and allow them to cool off. If desired, add aniseed liqueur just before serving.

Peel the potatoes and finely grate them with a fine grater. Add the semolina, a pinch of salt, cottage cheese and the egg and mix well. Allow the dough to rise for about 15 minutes.

Heat the butter in a frying pan. Fill the potato dough into the frying pan so that it is about 1 cm thick. Fry at medium heat for about 10 minutes, until underside is brown. Turn over and fry the other side for 5 minutes.

Using two forks, pull the potato pancake apart into smallish pieces and stir-fry them until they are crisp right round, add some more butter if necessary.

Serve the hot pancake pieces with the aniseed-apple sauce.

Frozen almond layer cake

Ingredients for 8–10 persons

For the cake
- 250 g peeled almonds
- 150 g icing sugar
- 2 egg whites

For the filling
- 3 eggs
- 200 g butter
- 60 g icing sugar
- 20 ml Amaretto (almond liqueur)
- 2 mocha-sized cups of very strong, cooled espresso
- 150 g bitter chocolate
- 3 T almond chips

If possible, bake the cake layers the day before serving. Pre-heat the oven to 150 °C (gas setting 1). Finely grind the 250 g peeled almonds and mix these with the icing sugar. Beat the 2 egg whites till they are stiff and fold them in.

Divide the dough into 3 portions. Place each portion between 2 layers of transparent foil and roll it out to fit the cake tin (Ø 24 cm). Bake the first layer on the middle shelf for 10-15 minutes and allow cooling. Bake the remaining 2 bases in the same way.

For the filling: Separate 3 eggs and whisk the egg whites until stiff. Beat the butter, egg yolks and icing sugar together till they are foamy. Stir in the beaten egg whites, tablespoon by tablespoon.

Blend the Amaretto with the cold espresso coffee. Soak an almond cake layer with 1/3 of this mixture.

Cover this cake-layer with 1/3 of the filling and spread it on evenly. Grate 50 g chocolate and sprinkle half of it over the filling. Carefully place another almond layer on top, soak the cake with 1/3 of the espresso-almond liqueur mixture, spread on the filling and sprinkle with chocolate as before. Repeat this procedure once more.

Cover the cake and stand it in a very cold fridge for 4 - 5 hours (or place it in a freezer for a shorter time). Before serving, generously scatter 100 g of roughly ground chocolate over the top. You could also decorate the cake with 3 tablespoons of almond chips.

Serve ice cold.

Fig tartlets with melon scoops

200 g puff pastry dough
8 ripe figs
125 ml cream
20 g liquid butter
1 vanilla pod (seeds & pulp)
40 g sugar
20 g custard or pudding powder
2 eggs
100 g apricot jam

For melons
500 ml strong red wine
50 ml red port
20 g sugar
1 orange
wheat starch for binding
1 Cavaillon melon, not too ripe

Roll out the pastry to the thickness of a knife back and line 8 tartlet tins (Ø 10 cm) with puff pastry so that the pastry is 1 cm higher than the tin. Cover the tins with tin foil, weigh it down with dried peas (or lentils, etc.) and bake blind at 220 °C in a pre-heated oven until golden yellow. Remove the foil and the legumes.

Peel the figs and cut them into slices of 0.5 cm thick. Decoratively lay out the pre-baked pastries.

Boil up the cream, butter, sugar and vanilla, and then beat in the custard powder and eggs. Pass the mixture through a sieve. Fill the cream mixture into the pastry cases and bake again at 220 °C till the filling solidifies. Remove from the oven and allow the tartlets to stand for 5-10 minutes. Pour in the rest of cream mixture and again, place it into the oven to solidify. Allow the tartlets to cool off and then glaze them with the liquid apricot jam.

For the melon balls: Boil up the red wine with port and sugar, and reduce the liquid to half. Peel the orange thinly and cut the peel into very fine strips (»Julienne«). Place the peels in cold water, boil up once, pour off the water and rinse off cold.

Add the Julienne orange strips to the reduced red wine and boil up briefly. Bind the red wine by stirring in dissolved wheat starch. Halve the melons, remove the seeds and scoop out 20 melon balls. Add the melon to the red wine sauce and simmer for 2-3 minutes.

Serve the warm fig tarts together with the melon balls.

Ricotta tartlets with strawberry sauce

Ingredients for 8 portions

Ricotta tartlets

2 sheets white gelatine
2 T milk
250 g ricotta
(Italian-style cream cheese)
50-75 g sugar
1 T sweet white wine
2 egg whites

Sauce

200 g aromatic strawberries
1-2 T sugar
2-3 T prickly pear liqueur

Soften the gelatine in cold water, press out the water and dissolve the gelatine by warming it in milk. Mix the ricotta and the sugar together and stir until creamy. Fold in the sweet white wine and finally stir in the dissolved gelatine. Whisk the egg whites till they are stiff and fold these into the ricotta. Spoon the mixture into lightly greased tartlet tins and cool in the fridge for 2 hours. Put the ingredients for the sauce into a saucepan, boil up for 5 minutes and blend in the mixer. Turn out the tartlets onto serving plates and spoon the strawberry sauce over the top.

White wine cake

For the dough

250 g wheat flour (type 405)
1 pinch baking powder
125 g cold butter
75 g icing sugar
1 sachet vanilla sugar
1 pinch salt
60 ml water

For the filling

150 g sugar mixed
with cinnamon powder
100 g wheat flour (type 405)
125 g cold butter
300 ml dry white wine

Knead the above ingredients into a dough and (if possible) allow cooling. Roll out the dough till it measures apx. 30 cm in diameter. Lay out the dough in a greased tart tin (Ø 26 cm) and trim the edges if necessary.
Mix the cinnamon powder into the sugar. Cover the base of the dough with several layers, alternating between the flour and the cinnamon-sugar. Cut the cold butter into cubes and distribute these on the dry ingredients. Pour the wine over and then bake in a pre-heated oven at 180°C (hot air convection) for about 40 minutes.

Hazelnut dumplings with liqueur apples

200 g hazelnuts
50 g flour
4 T cream
1 pinch salt
60 g sugar
4 eggs
2 large red apples
3 T lemon juice
1 large orange
125 ml prickly pear liqueur
60 g butter

Grind 150 g of the hazelnuts and cut 50 g into quarters and set these aside. Stirring continuously, roast the ground nuts in a pan without fat until they are light brown. In a bowl, mix the nuts with the flour, cream, a pinch of salt, a pinch of sugar and 2 eggs into a thick dough. Allow this dough to rise for 10 minutes, and then add the other 2 eggs.

Hold 2 tablespoons into hot water and then use these to form little dumplings from the nut-dough. Allow these to glide into lightly salted, boiling water and simmer for 10 minutes (do not boil). Remove and allow draining. To keep the dumplings warm, place them in a buttered dish and put them in the oven at 50 °C.

While the dumplings are cooking, rinse and peel the apples then quarter them, remove the cores and slice the apple. Trickle with lemon juice. Rinse the orange in hot water and peel one half very thinly, cut this peel into very thin strips and squeeze the orange.

Melt the sugar to a light brown caramel in a large frying pan. Add the apple slices, orange peel and juice, and cook the apples at a low setting for 3 – 5 minutes. Turn once. As soon as the orange syrup starts to thicken, add the liqueur and boil it up once more. Use a skimming ladle to remove the apples.

Serve the apples together with the hazelnut dumplings.

strawberry charlotte with a herb sauce & cinnamon grissini

400 g fresh Maltese strawberries, briefly rinsed and cut into small pieces
200 g fresh Maltese strawberries cut into thin slices
1 T honey
1 T prickly pear liqueur
1 tsp roasted sesame seeds
1 tsp »Kinnie« (Maltese orange-lemonade)
zest of 1 lemon
zest of 1 orange
2 mint leaves, finely chopped

For the sauce
2 T butter
2 T sugar
juice of 1 orange and 1 lemon
1 T honey
1 T herbal liqueur

Cinnamon grissini
100 g frozen puff pastry, cut into strips
150 g melted butter
1 T sugar
1 tsp ground cinnamon

Mix the strawberry pieces with the other ingredients and marinate.

For the sauce: Melt the butter then add the sugar and the honey. Pour in the juice and boil until the mixture thickens. Allow to cool and finally, pour in the herb liqueur.

Fry the pastry strips in the melted butter till golden yellow (at 180 °C). Drain on kitchen paper. Roll the pastry strips in a mixture of sugar and cinnamon.

Arrange the strawberry slices vertically in a circle (use a plastic ring with a diameter of 10 cm). Fill the marinated strawberries into the middle, and then remove the plastic ring.

Serve the strawberry charlotte with the sauce and the cinnamon sticks.

Peaches in an orange-caramel with amaretti cream

4 ripe peaches
250 g sugar
lemon juice
125 g crème fraîche (sour cream)
125 g orange juice
1 dash orange liqueur

Amaretti cream
125 g white cooking chocolate
1 vanilla pod
1 egg
1 T orange liqueur
1 sheet gelatine
250 ml whipping cream
50 g amaretti
(small dry Italian macaroons)

Skin the peaches by briefly placing them into boiling water and immersing them in cold water. Cut the peaches into segments.

Gradually pour the sugar into a large pan, caramelise by stirring constantly and occasionally add a few drops of lemon juice. Heat until the caramel is milk-coffee-brown. Stir in the crème fraîche, and then add the orange juice and the liqueur. Place the peaches in the hot orange caramel and allow drawing.

Carefully melt the cooking chocolate over a bain-marie. Whisk the egg, the contents of the vanilla pod and the liqueur over the bain-marie till foamy. Stir in the dissolved gelatine and gradually add the cooking chocolate to the egg and crème.

Whip the cream until it is stiff. Fold the cream and the and roughly cut-up amaretti bits to the other ingredients. Place the mixture in the fridge, either in a single dish or in 4 little bowls.

Decorate as desired with roasted sliced almonds, pistachios and orange peel.

Grilled apples with apple-olive oil sauce and olive jam

4 APPLES
60 ML OLIVE OIL,
FLAVOURED WITH CITRUS FRUIT
80 G SUGAR
2–3 LARGE ORANGES
4 T OLIVE PRESERVE

OLIVE JAM
50 G FRESH GREEN OLIVES
280 G BLACK OLIVES
200 G APPLES, DE-CORED
JUICE OF 1/3 LEMON
500 G SUGAR
3 SPRIGS LEMON-THYME
2 SPRIGS SAGE
1/2 SHEET GELATINE

For the jam: Make a cut into the fresh olives and soak them for 4 days, changing the water daily. Remove the stones from the black olives and soak them in water for 6 hours.

Peel the apples and cut them into chunks, drip some lemon juice onto the apple chunks and sprinkle sugar over them. Leave the apples to stand for at least an hour so that the juice can extract. Put all the ingredients into a copper jam pan and bring to boil. Allow to simmer till the setting point is reached (mixture develops popping bubbles). Leave to cool and then pour the jam into suitable jars.

Leave the other apples unpeeled, de-core and cut each into eight pieces, trickle citrus olive oil and sprinkle sugar over the eighths. Place them onto a baking tray and bake under the grill for apx. 10 minutes.

Peel and filet the oranges. Remove the white pith from some of the peel, cut these skins into fine strips and fry them lightly in a little olive oil.

Pour the juice created by the grilled apples into a saucepan, add some sugar and boil it down. If the apples did not let off much juice, add some commercial apple juice. When the juice has been reduced by about 3/4, blend half of it with the remaining oil.
Use the other half of the juice to dissolve the fond of the grilled apples, boil till the liquid is pale brown then add the juice left from fileting the oranges.

Arrange the apple and orange pieces on a dish. Dress with the apple-olive oil and the apple-orange sauce and garnish with a spoonful of the olive preserve in the centre. Decorate with the lightly fried strips of orange peel.

Maltese tiramisu with almond crust

For the biscuits (sponge fingers)
2 egg yolks
25 g icing sugar
2 egg whites
35 g sugar
contents of 1/2 vanilla pod
zest of 1/2 lemon
peel of 1/2 orange
75 g flour
2 T aniseed
icing sugar

For the Cocoa
200 ml milk
50 g sugar
100 g plain cooking chocolate
20 ml Amaretto liqueur

For the cream sauce
40 g roasted, grated almonds
150 ml milk
2 egg yolks
40 g sugar
4 sheets gelatine
20 ml Amaretto liqueur
120 g whipped cream
1 egg white
10 g sugar
1 pinch salt

4 T roasted sliced almonds

For the cocoa: Boil up the milk, add the sugar and the cooking chocolate and allow it to dissolve. Add the Amaretto and leave the cocoa to cool off.

For the sponge biscuits: Beat the egg yolks till they are frothy. Slowly add the icing sugar and beat again till the mixture is frothy.
Beat the egg white till it is semi-stiff, slowly add the sugar and continue beating till the mixture is very stiff.
Put the vanilla seeds, lemon and orange peel into the egg-yolk mixture, and then alternately fold in the sifted flour and the stiff egg whites.

Cover a baking tray with greaseproof paper and put the mixture into an icing bag with a nozzle. Squeeze out finger biscuits and sprinkle a few aniseeds on each biscuit, then sift a thick layer of icing sugar onto the biscuits and bake in preheated oven at 180 °C for apx. 10 minutes. Allow the biscuits to cool and tap off the excess sugar.

For the cream: Boil up the roasted almonds with the milk. Remove from the heat and leave to stand for 2 hours. Pour the milk through a fine sieve. Fill the almond-milk into a bain-marie (or stand the mixing bowl in hot water) and add the egg yolks and the sugar. Beat until creamy.
Beat the egg whites till stiff (include the salt and sugar).

Remove the gelatine from the cold water and press it out. Add the gelatine into the creamy mixture and stir till it dissolves. Remove the mixture from the bain-marie and whisk till it begins to turn solid. Add the Amaretto and stir till it is smooth, then fold in the whipped cream and the stiffened egg whites.

Spread half of the sponge biscuits in an oven dish and cover generously with cocoa. Allow the sponge to absorb the cocoa and then spread half the cream over. Distribute the rest of the biscuits thereon, and again, soak them with the remaining liquid chocolate and spread the remaining cream over. Scatter the tiramisu with a thick layer of sliced, roasted almonds. Keep in a cold place for apx. 3 hours.

Almond biscuits

170 g almonds
250 g flour
1 tsp baking powder
200 g sugar
1 vanilla pod (seeds & pulp)
1 pinch ground cardamom
1 pinch ground cinnamon
1 pinch ground star-anise
1 pinch ground cloves
1 pinch salt
1 T Amaretto
25 g soft butter
2 eggs

Blanche the almonds in boiling water for 1 minute. Pour through a sieve and turn out the almonds onto a kitchen cloth. Squeeze the almonds out of their skins (or buy peeled almonds).

Mix flour, baking powder, sugar, vanilla, cardamom, cinnamon, star-anise, cloves and a pinch of salt together in a bowl. Add the Amaretto, butter and eggs and using the kneading hooks on an electric hand-held mixer, knead the ingredients into a smooth dough. Knead at high speed, but not for too long; otherwise the dough will become too soft. Add the crushed almonds and knead them in. Form the dough into a ball and wrap it in transparent foil. Cool the dough for about 30 minutes.

Pre-heat the oven to 190 °C. Cut the dough into 5 pieces and roll each piece into a roll of 25 cm long. Lay out a baking tray with grease-proof paper. Place the rolls of dough onto the tray, leaving a space of 8 cm in between. Place the tray on the shelf 2nd from the bottom and pre-bake the rolls for 15 minutes. Allow cooling off slightly and then, using an electric carving-knife, cut off 1 cm thick diagonal slices. Lay out the biscuits on the baking tray and bake for another 8-10 minutes at 180 °C till the are golden brown.

Sesame biscuits

100 ml orange juice
200 g icing sugar
60 g flour
120 g liquid butter
125 g sesame seeds

Knead all the ingredients into smooth dough.

Pre-heat the oven to 200 °C. Place spoonfuls of the dough (keep wide spaces in between) onto the greaseproof paper on a baking tray and bake until golden brown.

Allow them to cool-off before removing the biscuits from the paper.

Lime cake with marinated, spicy oranges

For a rectangular cake tin (20 x 25 cm):

For the spicy oranges

- 5 oranges
- 130 g sugar
- 250 ml white wine
- 125 ml freshly squeezed orange juice
- 2 cardamom seeds
- 4 cloves
- 2 star-anises
- 2 cinnamon sticks
- 1 vanilla pod
- zest of 1 orange and 1 lemon
- 20 g corn starch
- 20 ml Grenadine
- 20 ml Grand Marnier

For the lime cake

- 125 g butter
- 125 g sugar
- 1 pinch salt
- zest of 1 lime and 1/2 orange
- 135 ml lime juice
- 100 g whole egg
- 125 g flour
- 7 g baking powder
- 125 g icing sugar
- 20 ml Grand Marnier

Filet the oranges. Caramelise the sugar, then stir in the white wine and boil for apx. 5 minutes before stirring in the orange juice. Add the spices and the citrus zests and allow to simmer for apx. 10 minutes.

Dissolve the corn-flour in a tablespoonful of cold water and add it to the orange-herb fond to bind. Boil up again briefly and allow cooling off.

Flavour with Grenadine and Grand Marnier, pour the mixture over the orange seg-ments and leave in the fridge to marinate for 1 day. Remove the spices before serving.

For the cake: Melt the butter and remove it from heat. Stir in 75 g of the sugar, salt and the zests of the lime and orange. Keep heating and stir until the mixture thickens, then stir in 35 ml of not too cold lime juice.

Pre-heat the oven to 180 °C.

Mix the whole egg with 50 g of sugar and heat up to 50 °C. Quickly, but briefly blend it in a kitchen mixer till the sugar is dissolved. Fold into the butter dough.

Whisk sifted flour and baking powder into the dough. Fill the dough into a tin lined with greaseproof paper and bake in the oven for apx. 30 minutes.

Mix 100 ml lime juice, the icing sugar and Grand Marnier and trickle the mixture over the freshly baked cake.

Rainer Mitze – the Star-Chef's career

Activities

1961–65 Apprenticeship and training at the Hotel Rosenhaus, Velbert

1965–67 Alexander Restaurant, Wuppertal

1967–68 Two Seasons in Westerland, Sylt

1968–70 Hotel Bermudiana, Bermuda

1970–80 the Oriental Hotel and the Dusit Thani Hotel, Bangkok

1980–99 Manager of the Executives' Restaurant and the kitchen of Bayer AG, Leverkusen

January 2000 Founded Rainer Mitze's Koch College

- A TV programme ZDF »Guten Appetit« with Johann Lafer
- A TV programme ZDF »Kochen wie in Asien« (»Cooking as in Asia«)
- A TV programme 3SAT »Frag Lafer«
- Culinary festival »East meets West«, in Burma and Bangkok (1996+97),
- Thailand (1995)
- Culinary reports for the »Gourmet« magazine and for the »Feinschmecker« magazine
- Jury Member at the Culinary Arts Competition Bangkok, 1992 – 1997 and Manila 1997–1999 – 2000
- Gala menu at the UN, New York ,1996 with the Federal Government (Dr. Klaus Kinkel, and others) and Johann Lafer
- Rhine Festival with LTU, Bangkok 1998
- Lecturer at the »Greystone« – The Culinary Institute of America – Nappa Valley, USA 1997 – 1999 – 2000
- A TV programme Vox TV »Kochduell« (»Ready, Steady, Cook«)
- Co-publisher of the culinary calendars »Euro-Asia Cuisine« 1994, »Desserts« 1995, »Desserts« 1996, »Fish« 1996, »Fish« 1997, »Game« 1998, and »Pacific« 1999
- Cooking college and gala menu, Aida club ship Caribbean tour 2001
- Gala menu, Coco Reef Resort Tobago (Trinidad), West Indies

Rainer Mitze's Koch College

Rainer Mitze's Koch College in Leverkusen, is open to people who wish to take the opportunity to discover the secrets of the culinary arts. In January 2000, the cookery college moved into the rooms in the monumental building in Dönhoffstraße. Here, Rainer Mitze has created a unique ambience, which immediately fascinates and inspires. The professionally equipped kitchen and the long dining table provide hobby chefs with enough space to prepare and enjoy the dishes together with the star chef. The courses introducing aspects of the Asian cuisine, are enjoying an increasing popularity, for which he draws his inspiration from the many years spent in the employment of the Oriental Hotel in Bangkok – the best hotel in the world. But the stylish rooms with their own digestive, cigar and Illy-coffee bars, as well as Mitze's Wine Bar are not only used by the cookery school, but also form an unusual setting for exclusive business lunches or dinners in a private atmosphere. Cooking, a sensual pleasure – these few words very aptly describe Rainer Mitze's philosophy. With a generous portion of

charm, wit and professionalism, Rainer Mitze brings the participants of his courses closer to the sensuality of cooking. This outstanding chef, who has received numerous awards from cuisine experts, and who became well-known through the German version of the »Ready, Steady, Cook« TV programme, not only values the food itself, but even more so the development of the finest dishes, in which no limits are set to your own creative skills.

Rainer Mitze's Koch College
Dönhoffstraße 19
51373 Leverkusen
Telephone ++49/214 – 8 40 50 80
Fax ++49/214 – 8 40 50 81

www.garcia.de/mitze
rm-kochcollege@t-online.de

INDEX

SOURCES OF SUPPLY

LIQUEURS:

Madalien Ltd.
Oratory Street
Naxxar NXR 03
Malta

Telephone: (+356) 21412391,
21431744
Fax: (+356) 21437129
info@madalien.info
www.madalien.info

WINE, SPARKLING WINE:

Marsovin Ltd.
The Winery
Wills Street
Marsa PLA 01
Malta

Telephone: (+356) 2182 4920
Fax: (+356) 21809501
info@marsovin.com.mt
www.marsovin.com

BEER, KINNIE:

Simonds Farsons Cisk plc
The Brewery
Mriehel BKR 01
Malta

Telephone: (+356) 23814206
Fax: (+356) 23814163
robertam@farsons.com
www.farsons.com
www.kinnie.com

WINE, BEER, LIQUEUR, KINNIE:

weinimport-24.de
Hans-W. Morawetz
Hembecker Talstraße 15 a
58256 Ennepetal
Germany

Telephone: (+49) 2333/76271
Fax: (+49) 2333/631899
hwmorawetz@morawetz.de
www.weinimport-24.de

Marsovin Ltd.
The Winery
Wills Street
Marsa PLA 01
Malta

Telephone: (+356) 2182 4920
Fax: (+356) 21809501
info@marsovin.com.mt
www.marsovin.com